Night Out

POEMS

ABOUT

HOTELS,

MOTELS,

RESTAURANTS,

AND BARS

Edited by Kurt Brown
and
Laure-Anne Bosselaar

MILKWEED
EDITIONS

Published 1997 by Milkweed Editions
Printed in the United States of America
Cover and interior art by David Lefkowitz
Cover design by Sarah Purdy
Interior design by Will Powers
The text of this book is set in Electra
97   98   99   00   01   5   4   3   2   1
First Edition

Milkweed Editions is a not-for-profit publisher. We gratefully acknowledge support from the Bush Foundation; Target Stores, Dayton's, and Mervyn's by the Dayton Hudson Foundation; General Mills Foundation; Honeywell Foundation; Jerome Foundation; The McKnight Foundation; Andrew W. Mellon Foundation; Minnesota State Arts Board through an appropriation by the Minnesota State Legislature; Challenge and Literature Programs of the National Endowment for the Arts; Lawrence and Elizabeth Ann O'Shaughnessy Income Trust in honor of Lawrence M. O'Shaughnessy; Piper Jaffray Companies, Inc.; Ritz Foundation; John and Beverly Rollwagen Fund of the Minneapolis Foundation; The St. Paul Companies, Inc.; Star Tribune/Cowles Media Foundation; Surdna Foundation; James R. Thorpe Foundation; Lila Wallace-Reader's Digest Literary Publishers Marketing Development Program, funded through a grant to the Council of Literary Magazines and Presses; and generous individuals.

Library of Congress Cataloging-in-Publication Data

Night out : poems about hotels, motels, restaurants, and bars / edited
    by Kurt Brown and Laure-Anne Bosselaar. — 1st ed.
        p.   cm.   14.95 ✓
    ISBN 1-57131-405-9 (alk. paper)
        1. American poetry—20th century.   2. United States—Social life
and customs—Poetry.   3. United States—Description and travel—
Poetry.   4. Bars (Drinking establishments)—Poetry.
    5. Restaurants—Poetry.   6. Hotels—Poetry.   7. Motels—Poetry.
    I. Brown, Kurt.   II. Bosselaar, Laure-Anne, 1943–
PS595.U5N54   1997
811'.5080355—dc21   96-47358
                                                       CIP

This book is printed on acid-free paper.

Night Out

To our children
Mathieu,
Maëlle,
and Maureen

Special Thanks

Emilie Buchwald of Milkweed Editions
for her continued friendship and expertise,
and to Dali Islam for her superb typing skills.

Special thanks to all those poets and
publishers whose cooperation and
wsupport helped make this book possible.

Extra-special thanks to Gerald Stern, David Rivard,
Jon Lavieri, Galway Kinnell, and W. D. Snodgrass
for going out of their way to assist us.

Night Out

Dining Late

Hamburger Heaven

Elysian Fields

Report from Nirvana

A PLACE IN THE PAST

THAT'S JAZZ

ALL OVER THE MAP

Preface

This is a superb collection of poems that encapsulates, in its way, the entire range of American feeling—our particular metaphysics, our transitoriness, our love of weeds and waste places, our despera- tion for the past, our regret and melancholy, our ridiculous bravery, our sexual yearning, our pride and shame, our ambiguity. I think our restaurants, motels, and watering places represent a kind of charged field where ordinary events—ordering a meal, spilling a lit- tle wine, remembering a certain bird—take on a significance that can only be called mythical, and that our writers, when they enter that field, know, instinctively by now, that they are in such a signifi- cant place.

So, in addition to the garden, wild or tamed, and that famous mountain near Athens, and that Book of Just Love, there is a new way of encountering the mystery and registering the adventure. It may be that this is our truest theater, and it may be that our grief and loneliness find the best focus, or a certain focus, only there. Certainly it is true that the bar and hotel poem has breathed life into a new kind of emotional encounter, just as it is true that certain emotions and experiences have been vitalized through this medium.

What is interesting is how contemporary a mode it is. Williams, in *Desert Music*, Auden in *Age of Anxiety* and "September 1st, 1939," Eliot in "Sweeney Among the Nightingales" anticipate it, but it had not, in their time, become the consuming metaphor, and even obses- sion, that it has become today. Indeed Auden, it seems to me, por- trays a kind of artfulness or self-consciousness, a delicious modernity as he observes the scene from the viewpoint of "one of the dives / on forty-second street" instead of, say, a bridge over the Thames or the front steps of a fourteenth-century cathedral.

There is sometimes in American poetry a straining after effect, often in cosmic, vegetal, and Olympian matters, almost the inverse of Auden, but in these poems there is no such straining. If anything is "natural" for an American poet it is the manner and matter, indeed the manna, of these poems, written—sometimes even literally—in hopelessly ugly and uncomfortable chairs, at small tables, in front of makeshift stages, in the middle of boring corridors, facing merciless clerks, hands over dead telephones or under lumpy pillows, fingers desperately pressing noisy air conditioners, eyes staring at ugly cracks and painted wires.

I am delighted by this collection, and I give thanks to Kurt and Laure-Anne.

Night Out

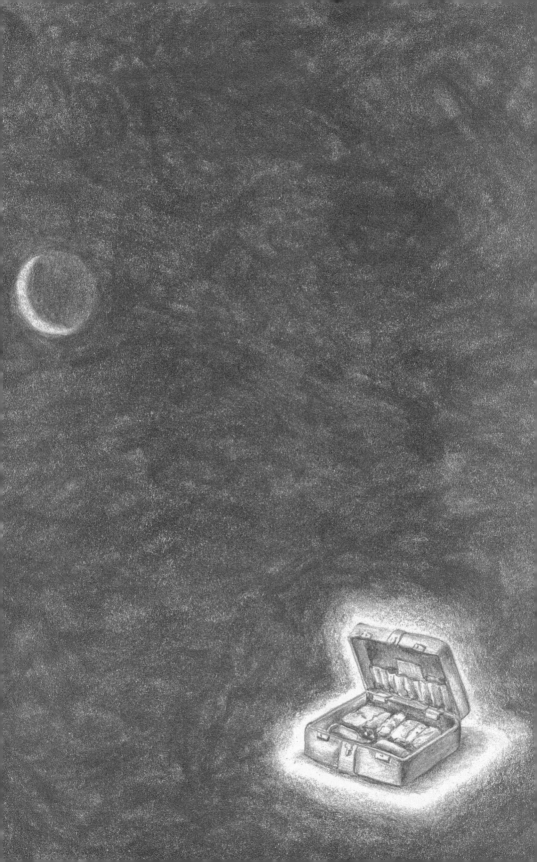

A Hotel by Any Other Name

"We have all been in rooms
We cannot die in, . . ."

JAMES DICKEY

By the Eastern Sea

SUSAN MITCHELL

The Hotel by the Sea

In the hotel by the sea a man is playing the piano.
The piano wants to be played
like a pinball machine, it wants the man to lean his weight
against the music until the sound tilts. But the man
wanders inside the piano like someone looking
for an elevator in a drafty building
or like a drunk who can't find
his way in a song he keeps repeating.

The piano wants to play leaky faucets and water running
all night in the toilets of a train station.
It wants to play obscenities
and the delicate moths that scratch their bellies
on the ballroom screens.
The piano wants to scratch. It wants to spit
on the pavement. It wants to look into stores where women
try on clothes and open their thighs to the mirrors.

The piano wants to be a fat woman. It wants to play
baggy and flab and carry tuna sandwiches to work
in brown paper. It wants to dress up in sequins and eat
fried fish. It wants to suck its fingers and flick
ashes into the ocean. And it wants to squeeze
into a single note,
a silvery tube, and hold its breath.
The piano tells the man to forget everything

he ever learned and play the music boys pass in secret
from desk to desk at school, the blue saliva
of their kisses. The man feels left out of
this music and thinks of going for cigarettes.
The piano wants to drink up
the butts littering the ballroom.
It wants to sit down on the dance floor
and sob with joy, it wants to rub

all memory of celebration from the man's fingers.
The piano wants to blow its nose
in the music and play the silence of the room and the rain
falling outside. It wants to play the pores
in the man's face and his chapped hands.
The piano wants the man to dance
in his sports shirt and floppy pants.
It wants him to ride up and down

the hotel elevators and follow women back
to their rooms. It wants him to pull roses from their hair
and mice and light up like an arcade.
The piano is sick and tired
of this man's hands which sit down
on their grief, as on a jetty, and count the stars.
The piano doesn't care about hard times.
It wants to stay up all night

and tell unrepeatable stories to the ocean.
It wants a sound to come
from this man's mouth, even though his teeth
are picked clean.
The man won't know the sound
when he makes it. He'll think a woman is kissing Kleenex.
He'll think it's 4 A.M. and he can't buy
a pack of anything anywhere.

CHARLES SIMIC

Hotel Insomnia

I liked my little hole,
Its window facing a brick wall.
Next door there was a piano.
A few evenings a month
A crippled old man came to play
"My Blue Heaven."

Mostly, though, it was quiet.
Each room with its spider in heavy overcoat
Catching his fly with a web
Of cigarette smoke and revery.
So dark,
I could not see my face in the shaving mirror.

At 5 A.M. the sound of bare feet upstairs.
The "Gypsy" fortuneteller,
Whose storefront is on the corner,
Going to pee after a night of love.
Once, too, the sound of a child sobbing.
So near it was, I thought
For a moment, I was sobbing myself.

Chanel No. 5

Life had become a sort of gorgeous elegy,
intimate with things about to be lost.

The waiter's hand on the wineglass
seemed an intermediary flame,

the atoms rampant inside it,

though it moved slowly
and hesitated slightly
before it was withdrawn

as if it meant to ask
whether anything more was wanted.

Abstracted by the static of the surf,

I dined alone, the beach hotel
half empty in the off-season,

the honeymooning couple
at the table next to mine

caressing with their voices
the still-folded map of their future,

their two armies still in reserve,

the flowers massed between them
a flimsy barricade
against their wakening grief.

The long pin of her corsage
pierced the thin silk on her breast:
white flower, green leaf, black dress.

In her perfume I smelled
the residue of all their recent happiness,
a sweetness corrupted by the sea, and yet

she wore it innocently, that target.

It was fledgling bitterness I caught
off a shred of air that had touched her dress
as she rose to follow her husband-mystery.

The little emblem inside the flame,
the male and female become one,

was blackening back in their room

overlooking the sea, but before they
hurried back to it, she looked at me,
and, as if to inoculate herself against me,

inclined her head to smell her own gardenia.

PETER E. MURPHY

At the Waterloo Hotel

Here dreams are interrupted by a woman
who screams so loudly she cracks open your death-like sleep,
yet fails to ruffle security or the front desk
which never answers the telephone, never responds.
So you bang on that awful door that wails *Stop it.*
You're hurting me! Stop! and it finally stops.

Later when sleep is again broken by the persistent tapping
on your door, you pull on your pants and look through the peephole
at the nightgowned woman who startles when you crack it open,
is confused when you say *Yes?* She doesn't realize
she's walked in her sleep in a hotel known for its exotic obscurity,
its Victorian sense of loss, it's love-thin doors and walls.

As she sleep stumbles toward other rooms
you close your door and wonder if hers were the screams
that had earlier awakened you.
You wonder if she moves toward abuse or toward love
that doesn't bruise, love that sleeps in a lost room
unaware she is searching among all the locked doors.

You return to your bed so exhausted you hurt
and lie there for hours in stubborn wakefulness,
practicing over and over how to close your eyes,
how to keep them closed, practicing till you finally turn
away from the stony light into the rising darkness
of your own rooms.

JAMES HAUG

Terminal Hotel

There's always a vacancy here.
A doorman under the ragged canopy
wears his heart out, waiting
decades for a crimson Packard,
and rubs the eagle clean
off a silver dollar.
He's been witness to Prohibition,
the Red Scare, and urban renewal —
and now you, stepping down,
uncertain in the glare of departing
buses, the bag at your feet
caved in like a broken hat,
empty of everything you knew
you wouldn't need but the fake
beard and the i.d. of someone
who looks just like you.
It is midday. The sun fires
the color right out of your eyes,
sidewalk hot enough to fry.
You want lemonade, a good smoke.
You sit in the chair and rest
a foot on the metal step. A boy
bends over your shoe and applies
black polish, then the stained chamois.
In this kind of heat you realize
it could take forever: the boy
muttering over your wing tips,
the doorman's pocket full of change.

Jackson Hotel

Sometimes after hours of wine I can almost see
        the night gliding in low off the harbor
                down the long avenues of shopwindows

past mannequins, perfect in their gestures.
        I leave water steaming on the gas ring
                and sometimes I can slip from my body,

almost find the single word to prevent evenings
        that absolve nothing, a winter lived alone
                and cold. Rooms where you somehow marry

the losses of strangers that tremble
        on the walls, like the hands
                of the dancer next door luminous

with Methedrine; she taps walls for hours
        murmuring about the silver she swears
                lines the building, the hallways

where each night drunks stammer their
        usual Rosary until they come to rest
                beneath the tarnished numbers, the bulbs

that star each ceiling.
        I must tell you I am afraid to sit here
                losing myself to the hour's slow erasure

until I know myself only by this cold weight,
        this hand on my lap, palm up.
                I want to still the dancer's hands

in mine, to talk about forgiveness
        and what we leave behind—faces
                and cities, the small emergencies

of nights. I say nothing but,
     leaning on the sill, I watch her leave
          at that moment

when the first taxis start rolling
     to the lights of Chinatown, powered
          by sad and human desire. I watch her fade

down the street until she's a smudge,
     violet in the circle of my breath. A figure
          so small I can cup her in my hands.

Transients Welcome

"Transients Welcome"

To be like the water:
a glass snake asleep in the pipes.
But behind you the dream burns the empty nests,
and before you the day with its ball of twine.

You piss in the sink. Frying pan in hand,
padding down the hall, you turn the corner
and find an old woman asleep on the stove.

Hotel St. Louis, New York City, Fall 1969

When I went inside, the manager said, "You don't want to live here, kid." And even naïve as I was I could see, looking at the people in the lobby, it was a violent place. I told him I didn't have much money and he said, "This place is for junkies and hoods; go to the St. Louis—that's winos and they're harmless," and he wrote out an address and slipped it under the bulletproof plastic window that covered his small booth.

He was right: in the five months I lived there, no one ever harmed me. I got an 8-by-10 room with a bed, a sink, and a dresser for $15 a week. That left me twenty for food.

My room was on the second floor, with a window on the air shaft. Next door, in an identical room, lived a bedraggled redhead named Beatrice Tiffany and her boyfriend Joe, a security guard. Whenever I caught a glimpse of him staggering, bleary-eyed and unshaven, down the narrow hall in his gray uniform and thick black belt, I prayed he wasn't allowed to carry a gun on the job, or, worse yet, to bring one home. Tiffany's grown son, Eddie, and his boyfriend, Albert, lived in that tiny room too, sleeping on a mat on the floor.

What separated us was so thin it was more like a veil than a plaster wall. Whatever happened in their world happened in mine.

Luckily, we were on different schedules: working six nights a week in a bookstore, I missed most of their family dramas. Mornings, when I was in, my neighbors were either sleeping it off or gone. I'd wake around six, piss in the sink, then boil water for coffee on the stove at the end of the hall.

All morning, I worked on my writing: drafts of poems, dream narratives, stray ideas. Around noon, I'd make two peanut-butter sandwiches, then, in midafternoon, leave for work. In the evening at the bookstore, I'd have a ham-and-cheese sandwich, a piece of pound cake, and a carton of milk. I never varied that routine, telling myself the lettuce in my deli sandwich was the daily green I needed and that the milk made it a balanced diet. Still, I lost two teeth that fall; they simply crumbled and fell out.

One week I was working on an idea to strengthen my memory by going back to the house where I lived when I was ten. Sitting on my hotel bed, I'd close my eyes and be standing on the front walk. To my right was the mountain ash with its orange berries; behind me, to the left, my mother's gray-and-white Chevy parked under the huge weeping birch whose feathery branches brushed its roof. As I walked up the steps I saw the white lattice of the porch and the hole beneath it where the dogs had burrowed. I entered and walked from room to room, pausing every few feet to notice as many details as I could: the worn cane seat of a chair, the color and pattern of a hooked rug my mother had made, the cover of a particular book in the library.

I could only make this journey twenty minutes at a time before my head started to buzz and I had to stop. Each day that week, I repeated my walk, concentrating on a different room and remembering more details each time. There was only a single place—one whole wall of the living room—where I couldn't see anything and found myself wincing and turning away no matter how many times I tried to look.

Late that week I woke up knowing I'd lost control of my mind. Thoughts whizzed by and my head felt light and impossibly intense. This had been my goal—to change my consciousness, but now that it had happened I was terrified. The last small voice of sanity said: "Don't panic. Get food. Food will bring you down."

I fled the hotel to find a coffee shop. As I passed the supermarket on Broadway, a man in a butcher's white smock yelled "Watch out!"

and pushed by me with a silver shopping cart in which stood the entire carcass of a lamb, complete with blind eyes in a bloody head.

I ate and felt calmer; returned to the hotel, slept, and woke feeling normal. Next door, I heard Albert telling Beatrice how he'd walked ninety blocks to the Village to sell his blood, only to discover it was Saturday and the place was closed, so he turned around and walked back and now his feet hurt. Albert's voice sounded flayed and blank as the dead lamb's face, and I found myself saying out loud: "How can anyone so dumb survive?" But he did, of course; we all did somehow.

I slept again, and when I woke it was late that night and the whole hotel was partying. From all ten floors, confusion of loud musics and slurred shouts and, in the air shaft, the whistle and crash of empty wine jugs dropped from a hundred windows.

When I woke from my third sleep, it was morning and I heard the black janitor with his push broom in the alley, clearing a path through our jagged garden of glass. He worked quietly and quickly, and he wore, as he always did on Sunday mornings, a bright orange football helmet that glowed like the sun.

TED KOOSER

Boarding House

The blind man draws his curtains for the night
and goes to bed, leaving a burning light

above the bathroom mirror. Through the wall,
he hears the deaf man walking down the hall

in his squeaky shoes to see if there's a light
under the blind man's door, and all is right.

DIONISIO D. MARTÍNEZ

Dancing at the Chelsea

It is no longer a question of balance and yet
we dance to keep from falling.

We dance because the rough
surface of the moon has carved a hole in the dark.

We dance on the beams of our unfinished houses.
We were dancing when our real houses

vanished and our lives became this.
We dance because this thin European found

a piano in the hall and dragged it
into his room, and we had to celebrate

the way he dragged it in by himself
and the way he hacked at the keys like mad.

We are still dancing, still celebrating.
We dance with the ghost of Sid

Vicious in the elevator.
We were dancing before the murder.

We were dancing in the lobby when we heard
something and we all

felt a sharp pain and we thought it was only
our tired and reluctant muscles giving

up on our bodies. Now
we dance for the limousine driver and his family,

we dance for the genius, for the man
with a hole in his head, for the one who has

lived here forever.
We dance for every song ever

written about these rooms.
We dance full of vertigo looking

down from any window above 23rd Street,
we let ourselves

go like scarves in a confused wind.
We will be dancing after the man with

the hole in his head has burned
perfect circles through the soles of his shoes.

We will dance on the broken bones
of our feet. We think

we can go on even as ghosts, as angels looking
down at the blessing of 23rd Street.

We climbed the stairs dancing
the night of the blackout when the elevator

stopped. This was long before the ghost.
We still dance when we climb

and descend the stairs. We still
use the stairs because we like the romance of it.

We've danced through every modern war.
We dance

each night after the last club has closed down
like a war no one knows how to end and all

that remains is a scratched record and someone
humming and the inevitable piano

and all the lost angels in the halls.
We will be dancing when the last

angel cuts his own wings off and tosses them
to the moon and jumps like another

blessing from any window above 23rd Street.
We dance in spite of gravity and the failure

of perpetual motion, in spite of the sleepless
angels of mathematics.

We dance the dance of those who speak
in tongues.

We dance like the shadows
of puppets in someone's clumsy hands. Sometimes

we dance with our own clumsy shadows.
We dance to keep from falling in love with

the lives of the strangers we
picked when the lights went out. Some

of us lit candles. Remember? But this
was after the fact. In the dark

we had changed partners and now
we found ourselves clinging to strange

new lives. We knew
that it would be like this from here on.

We would dance
and dance, hoping that through friction

or obsolescence or possibly even perfect
balance we would rid ourselves

of these lives. This, at least,
was the hope that kept us dancing.

The truth was something else. We knew
that we would change partners again

and again like bums trading stolen
goods by the light of the small fire they've

made in the aisle of an abandoned Pullman.

Transient Hotel Sky at the Hour of Sleep

On the late shift, front desk,
midnight to 8 A.M.,
we watched the sky through crusted windows,
till the clouds swirled away
like water in the drain
of a steel sink.

In the clouded liquid light
human shapes would harden,
an Army jacket staggering
against the bannister at bartime,
coal-skinned man
drifting through the lobby
moaning to himself
about Mississippi,
a known arsonist
squeezing his head
in the microwave oven
with a giggle.

As we studied the white face
of the clock above the desk,
fluorescent hum of 4 A.M.,
a cowboy bragged
about buying good boots
for 19 cents from a retarded man,
then swaggered out the door
with a pickaxe
and a treasure map.
The janitor mopped the floor
nostalgic for Vietnam snapshots
confiscated at the airport,
peasant corpses with jaws
lopsided in a song of missing teeth.

Slowly the sky was a comfort,
like the pillow of a patient
sick for decades
and sleeping at last.
At the hour of sleep
a man called Johnson
trotted down the hallway
and leaned out the window,
then again, haunting
the fifth floor
in a staring litany
of gestures, so even
the security guard on rounds
wrote in the logbook for social workers
who never kept a schedule at night.
Johnson leaped
through the greasy pane of sky
at 5 A.M.,
refused suicide in flight,
and kicking struggled to stand in the air,
but snapped his ankles on the sidewalk
and burst his head on the curb,
scalp flapped open like the lid
on a bucket of red paint.

The newspaper shocked mouths
that day, but the transient hotel sky
drained pale as usual,
and someone pissed in the ashtray
by the desk, then leered
at the jabbering smokers.

Rented Pleasures

Desire

There is a small wrought-iron balcony . . .
& at that balcony she stood a moment
Watching a summer fog
Swirl off the river in huge
Drifting pockets as the street lights grew
Alternately muted then wild then to a blurred
Relay of yellow

Her hair was so blond that from a distance
It shone white as spun silk
& as he turned the corner he stopped suddenly
Looking up at the window of the hotel room
Where she stood in her Japanese kimono
Printed with red dragonflies
& a simple bridge

& in that lapse of breath
As the fog both offered & erased her in the night
He could remember every pulse of her tongue
Every pared detail of constancy left
Only to them as he began
Walking slowly toward the door of the hotel
Carrying the hard loaf of day-old bread
& plums wrapped in newspaper

Already remembering this past he would desire

CHASE TWICHELL

Worldliness

When I close my eyes,
the wind upbraids the dusk and snow
outside our room, fifteen floors
above the frozen park. Drink in hand,
he lies back in an open robe,
changing the channels by remote control.
The hotel's heating system blurts
sporadic clouds into the faint
geometry of unlit monoliths
beyond a flimsy Spanish balcony.
That, of all things, is what I see.

When the story finally ends,
the stray heart wanders home
to twitch in its sleep before the fire,
rummaging again through all the secret
rooms in which it was powerful and whole,
circling and circling its one conclusion,
which is not the story's conclusion.
So that now, elsewhere,
in harmless, flowering weather,
I wake in a steep-sided daydream
as a swimmer wakes in a wave.

☽

I said, Men dream, but they go home.
Did that make me the devil,
me with my small-scale recklessness?
It was easy to see what he wanted:
the violent litheness of the young,

heir mother-deafness.
When I spoke I think he heard

some of the sad music of his youth.
The car that loved the streets
of adolescence, the first wife

darkening in Italy among stone
fountains, ruins, historic flowers.
He was so . . . impermanent,
my newly made, my middle-aged roué,
my randy dreamer sliding through

a foxtrot cheek to cheek with alcohol.
I knew we could not go on sleeping forever
in the thin tent of the present tense,
and that the ink would someday feather away
from these words as if bent on escape.

I knew, and yet I lay down
in the sanctuary of the intellect
and took off my clothes there.
How could he deny me? He wanted
to change his life in my body.

☾

The flip side of a wish is a fear,
and that was why we crushed
the heaven from those darkened rooms.

How easily the stubborn pearl
hoarded up and gave away
its infinite concentric mysteries,

how easily, how many times,
the nipples tightening, the mouth
wet muscle in the intimate marine.

We rode for a brief time
the salty violet undertow,
able to will the drowning we desired,

a liquid slide over the world's brink
in a rush of holy tremblings.
Once, undone by the threshing beauty

of our bodies, I imagined myself suddenly
naked in the restless cold cascades
of Taylor's Flume in the moonlight,

slipping with all my boy cousins
down through the bolts of darkness,
the waterfall loud and the rocks clean,

working our way against the muscular
currents, chased by the half-fear,
new to us then, for which I would

someday risk my accumulated self.
We swam as though the future
flowed around us, clean and cold,

but that was childhood—
pure, implacable, and long ago.
I meet him there, in the past,

where there are other names
for the heart in love with the arrow,
names for the spirit in the white pulse.

I go back, I meet him there,
whatever he asks me to do, I do.
I close my eyes,

and taste the cloudy caviar,
and hear outside whatever hotel
and metrically stupid traffic.

☾

I want to love the story of my life,
the stories. Then I shall seem
not so much a creature in an index
of adventures or of dreams

as an interactive force that fed itself
on love, a force that did not atrophy.
And if it was reckless,
what will it matter?

I did what I did
for the sake of intensity,
and I am unrepentant
even in my emptiness.

☾

Once, when I slipped in my robe
down the hotel corridor
to the ice machine at 2 A.M.,

what I thought was a boy
turned, his bucket full of glassy cubes,

but instead it was a half-sized man,
stopped in the face and chest,
his day's beard a blue rasp.

I saw us in the plate glass,
behind which snow was falling.

He backed me up against the ice machine

and pressed his unimaginable little
torso against me, but his heart beat so
anonymously hard that I forgave him.

Adultery

We have all been in rooms
We cannot die in, and they are odd places, and sad.
Often Indians are standing eagle-armed on hills

In the sunrise   open wide to the Great Spirit
Or gliding in canoes   or cattle are browsing on the walls
Far away   gazing down with the eyes of our children

Not far away   or there are men driving
The last railspike, which has turned
Gold in their hands. Gigantic forepleasure lives

Among such scenes, and we are alone with it
At last. There is always some weeping
Between us   and someone is always checking

A wrist watch by the bed to see how much
Longer we have left. Nothing can come
Of this   nothing can come

Of us: of me with my grim techniques
Or you who have sealed your womb
With a ring of convulsive rubber:

Although we come together,
Nothing will come of us. But we would not give
It up, for death is beaten

By praying Indians   by distant cows   historical
Hammers   by hazardous meetings that bridge
A continent. One could never die here

Never die   never die
While crying. My lover, my dear one
I will see you next week

When I'm in town. I will call you
If I can. Please get hold of   please don't
Oh God, Please don't any more I can't bear . . . Listen:

We have done it again   we are
Still living. Sit up and smile,
God bless you. Guilt is magical.

A Hotel by Any Other Name

Love—even forbidden love—doesn't deserve linoleum,
doesn't expect to pay cash up front to an experienced
frown behind bullet-proof glass; but this magnetism
is discovered on the fly, in a city neither can claim.
Not sure how to get their hands into the act but knowing

it will happen, they walk, boiling down their lives,
comparing reactions to curbside offerings and moulting
neighborhoods, nibbling nuts and the idea of other.
Forty blocks, fifty, and they are as good as undressed.
Laughing, they watch their shoes lead them here, to hotel

resolute, hotel no-nonsense on the square: no luggage, no soap,
no telling. They don't need a lobby with "Moon River."
They pump their bodies like the necks of young swans,
gleeful to sweat on bad beds under worse art, mopping their
sweet new juice with holey towels thin as the walls,

which all night amplify moaning and showers, fisticuffs
and redemption. None of it pedigreed, all of it audible,
memorex, like their love. A hotel in the middle of otherwise,
which will stand—squat and sure on this rubbled and unsuspecting
street and nowhere else, it will stand, clapping.

Gem Inn, Kandy

for Peter

This is the window in a wall of windows in the room
where we lay down beside the end of summer. This
the fine thrum of a car in the distance. And this
moonlight, like the pool of a gown fallen on the floor,
is the diva's aria. This is the poem, liquid
by Tagore. This the bolt lock on the door.

This is the bed, made by sliding two beds together.
This the hour, where side by side, we spoke
a language we had not dared speak before. And this
the scent of plumeria, redolent on the air,
sharp as rare metal. This is the opening into
the lair of an animal, and this is your hand

there. Here, I sing the recitative
of everything we did together in that room, in another
country. Now my mouth, closed around silence:
whom will it kiss? To whom whisper? Tell me
one thing sweeter than the whispering of two friends
who have found each other after long, diligent

loneliness. There is no elixir like this,
this glass half full of light, half full of dark.

JORIE GRAHAM

In the Hotel
(3:17 A.M.)

Whir. The invisible sponsored again by white
walls—a joining in them and then (dark spot)
(like the start of a thought)
a corner, fertilized by shadow, hooked, dotted,
here demurring, there—up there—
almost hot with black. . . . What time is it?
The annihilation. The chaste middle of things.
Then I hear them, whoever they are, as if
inside my wall, as if there were a multitude of tiny wings
                                        trapped
inside the studs and joints.
The clockdial hums. Greenish glow and twelve stark dots
round which this supple, sinewed, blackest flesh
must roil—vertebrate. A moaning now—a human moan—and then
another cry—but small—
furry in the way the wall can hold it—no
regret—a cry like a hypothesis—another
cry—the first again?—but not as in
dialogue—no—no question in it,
no having heard—now both—no moods in that room—
no fate—cries the precipitate of something on the verge of—
all of it supple now, threadbare in this black we share,
little whelps, vanquishings, discoveries, here under this
                                        rock,
no, over here, inside this sky, or is it below?—paupers,
                                        spoors—
a common grave—the backbone still glowing green—
and blackness, and the sense of walls, and the voicing they
provide, and my stillness here—unblinking—I am almost
                                        afraid
to move—and the litheness of this listening—
gossipy murmuring syllables now rushing up the scales,
but not really towards, not really away,

as if the thing deepened without increase,
the weight of the covers upon me,
the weight of the black, the slack and heaving argument
                              of gravity—

and her quavering, lingering—
and him—what had been mossy
                suddenly clawed—
and everything now trying to arrive on time, ten thousand
                      invisible things all
braided in, fast—*appetite, the clatter of wheels upon tracks,
the rustling—what did I lose?—what was it
like?*—the weight of covers now upon me like the world's
                              shut lid,

shut fast—not opening—
and cries, and cries, and something that will not come true.
When I stand up, pulling the heavy bedclothes back,
I want to open up the black.
Water sounds in the pipes between us.
A raised voice. Some steps.
More water in the singing pipes.
And scuffling. And the clicking of their light going off . . .
Debris of silences inside the silence.
Black gorged with absences. Room like an eyelid
                      spanked open
wide, I rip it, I rip it further—as if inside it now the million
tiny slippages could go to work, the whistling
                      of absence
where the thing *should care for us*—
where justice shifts and reshifts the bits to make
                      tomorrow—
tirelessly—kingdom of scribble and linger. . . . What do you
want, *you*, listening here with me now? Inside the
                      monologue,

what would you insert? What word?
What mark upon the pleating blackness of hotel air?
What, to open it? To make it hear you. To make it hear me.
How heavy can the singleness become?
Who will hear us? What shall we do?
I have waited all this time in the sooty minutes,
green gleaming bouquet offering and offering itself
right to my unrelenting open eyes,
long black arm tendering its icy blossoms up to me,
right through the blizzard of instances, the blurry
blacknesses, the whole room choked with the thousand spots
                              my glance has struck—
Long ago, long ago, and then, second-hand, this place
                              which is now,
whir—immortal? free?—glances like flames licking the walls . . .
Oh blackness, I am your servant. I take for mine your green, exactest
                              gift
in which you say yourself, in which you say
only yourself—

Hotel Lenox

And she loved loving
So she woke and bloomed
And she rose.

And many men had been there
To drowse awake and go downstairs
Lonely for coffee and bread.

But she drowsed awake lonely
For coffee and bread.

And went upstairs
With me, and we had
Coffee and bread.

And then we were so happy to see the lovely
Mother who had been her mother a long time.

In this city broken on the wheel

We went back to the warm caterpillar of our hotel.

And the wings took.

Oh lovely place,

Oh tree.

We climbed into the branches
Of the lady's tree.

We birds sang.

And the lemon light flew out over the river.

PETER E. MURPHY

At the Meadowlands Hotel

On this discounted weekend a yahoo threatens sleep
with a stadium voice in the midnight corridor, fumbling
for keys, needing to go and getting nowhere, he takes time out
to pee in the hallway, yelling, "Had to be done. Couldn't be helped!"
And later, his laughing date with a cheerleader's talent for whooping,
runs play after play against the headboard wall,
my wall on the other side, trying to keep the ball
alive until his beer-slowed goal is scored.
And me on the line between sleep and wakefulness, stupor
and fury, seek the front desk to referee and get transferred
to a new room on another floor, another view.

This morning the wind moves tons of bare branches
through a forest of snow flurries. Magnificent!
How the sun gets fired and runs through, deflecting
each flake, flustering their silver sides up, knocking
their crazy Xs and Os all over the rolling sky till they land,
forming a lightning glaze over the courtyard, a glaze that turns
the green field of the swimming-pool cover silver, a glaze
that recovers all sleeplessness, a glaze that allows morning
to defeat the offenses of the night before.

Way Out West

The Hotel du Nord

On the lawn of the old hotel at twilight
a boy stands swathed in a white towel,
his hair still damp from the lake.
The lamps come on
with precocious nostalgia.
Crickets resume in the folds of darkness,
and a boat left empty at the dock
knocks in the negligible waves.
Others have stopped at a spot like this
to listen to a lake's consoling messages.
Through decades of summers
their lowered voices abide,
filtered through the subsequent silences
of love withheld,
or the lies administered
to small ongoing arguments
like fresh bandages, to soothe them.
We stood there too, in northern Wisconsin
in the steadiness of summer,
our children unborn,
our love for one another boundless.
Looking back now
into the vacant twilight of a snapshot,
a reach of fragrant lawn —
the ordinary present darkens
in the tinctures of the past.
But I would not go back to see
the Hotel du Nord loom up again,
its innocent porches, its balconies of hope,
knowing that the paths beside the lake
all lead here, to the one place.
There is no elsewhere.

STEPHEN DUNN

Belly Dancer at the Hotel Jerome

Disguised as an Arab, the bouzouki player
introduces her as Fatima, but she's blond,
midwestern, learned to move we suspect
in Continuing Education, Tuesdays, some hip
college town.
We're ready to laugh, this is Aspen
Colorado, cocaine and blue valium
the local hard liquor, and we
with snifters of Metaxa in our hands,
part of the incongruous
that passes for harmony here.
But she's good. When she lets her hair loose,
beautiful. So we revise:
summer vacations, perhaps, in Morocco
or an Egyptian lover, or both.
This much we know:
no Protestant has moved like this
since the flames stopped licking their ankles.
Men rise from dinner tables
to stick dollar bills where their eyes
have been. One slips a five
in her cleavage. When she gets to us
she's dangling money
with a carelessness so vast
it's art, something perfected, all her bones
floating in milk.
The fake Arabs on bongos and bouzouki are real
musicians, urging her, whispering
"Fatima, Fatima," into the mike
and it's true, she has danced the mockery out
of that wrong name in this unlikely place,
she's Fatima and the cheap, conspicuous dreams
are ours, rising now, as bravos.

MARK IRWIN

The Western Hotel
(Ouray, Colorado)

People sip drinks below a mountain lion
pawing the air for a grouse, and you can still feel
easy walking upstairs to your room, where the grander idea
of history slips off its clothes. Sleep's easy
at this altitude, too. Downstairs, the cellar
snores nightmare: what the coal-loading furnace

knows as logic's ground: a secret tunnel
to the prostitutes' cribs. How easy one's tempted from
cold! The embalming table recalls
how one wise hotel owner respected both kinds
of sleep, first pickling his guests upstairs
with whiskey, then years later with formaldehyde

stored in gallon cans right above shelves
of Mason Jars. Apricots and mountain prunes
still carry the river water of a hundred-year's
past-cold. Business was good! What's
this?—Some old taxidermist tools? Framed photos
of mining camps, everywhere: Yankee Boy,

Imogene, Telluride. Against so much gray
the whites of their eyes drill stars,
constellations named Hope, Lust-for-Earth,
Strength, Greed. And here's a trunkful of old leather
bibles. Once, each held down a room. And here's
a child's tiny casket, large and empty as a mine.

RICHARD HUGO

What the Brand New Freeway Won't Go By

The block is bare except for this five-story
ugly brick hotel. Perhaps the bulk
frightened stores and homes away. Age is clear
in turrets and the milk on window sills.
The new name and the outside coat of paint
must have raised the rent. As you drive by
the rooms seem yellow and the air inside
is stale because a roomer, second floor,
in underwear, unshaven, fries a meal.

To live here you should be a friend of rain,
and fifty with a bad job on the freights,
knowing the freeway soon will siphon
the remaining world away
and you can die unseen among your photos—
swimmers laughing but the day remembered cold.

Rooms have gas. The place was in the papers.
Police have issued statements about cancer
and the case is closed, but not the jokes
passing boys are drilling through the walls.
Top-floor renters look down floors of sweat
to traffic that might stop were they to go.
Some rooms are paid for in advance with shock.

If, when the freeway opens, a man
afraid of speed still takes this road,
the faded Under New Management sign
might mean to him: we are older too—
live here—we'll never treat you badly again.

W. S. MERWIN

The Hotel-Keepers

All that would meet
The eyes of the hawks who slid southward
    Like paired hands, year after year,
Over the ridge bloody with autumn
    Would be the two iron roofs,
House and barn, high in the gap huddled,
    Smoke leaking from the stone stack,
A hotel sign from one hook dangling,
    And the vacant wagon-track
Trailing across the hog-backed mountain
    With no other shack in sight
For miles. So an ignorant stranger
    Might rein up there as night fell
(Though warned by his tired horse's rearing
    At nothing near the barn door)
And stopping, never be seen after;
    Thus pedlars' wares would turn up
Here and there minus their lost pedlars;
    Hounds nosing over the slope
Far downwind would give tongue suddenly
    High and frantic, closing in
On the back door; and in the valley
    Children raucous as starlings
Would start behaving at the mention
        Of the Hotel-Man.

Who was not tall,
Who stumped slowly, brawny in gum-boots,
    And who spoke little, they said
(Quarrymen, farmers, all the local
    Know-it-alls). Who was seen once,
When a nosey passer-by followed
    Low noises he thought were moans,
Standing with raised axe in the hayloft,

And whose threats that time, although
Not loud, pursued the rash intruder
    For months. But who, even so,
Holed up in his squat house, five decades
    Outwintered the righteous wrath
And brute schemes they nursed in the valley,
    Accidents, as they well knew,
Siding with him, and no evidence
    With them. And survived to sit,
Crumpled with age, and be visited
    Blabbing in his swivel-chair
With eyes adrift and wits dismantled,
    From sagging lip letting fall
Allusions of so little judgment
    That his hotel doors at last
Were chained up and all callers fielded
        By his anxious wife.

            A pleasant soul
Herself, they agreed: her plump features
    Vacant of malice, her eyes
Hard to abhor. And once he was crated
    And to his patient grave shrugged
(Where a weedy honor over him
    Seeded itself in no time)
They were soon fetching out their soft hearts
    To compare, calling to mind
Sickness, ruffians, the mountain winter,
    Her solitude, her sore feet,
Haling her down with all but music,
    Finally, to the valley,
To stand with bared gums, to be embraced,
    To be fussed over, dressed up
In their presents, and with kind people

Be settled in a good house,
To turn chatty, to be astonished
    At nothing, to sit for hours
At her window facing the mountain,
    Troubled by recollections
No more than its own loosening stream
    Cracking like church pews, in spring,
Or the hawks, in fall, sailing over
            To their own rewards.

Hotel Sierra

The November air
Has curled the new leaves
Of the spider plant, strung
From an L-bent nail
Driven in the warp of the window
Frame. Maybe the woman down
At the desk has a few more opinions—
On the dying plant, or the high
Bruised clouds of the nearing storm,
Or the best road
Along the coast this time of year
To Oregon. This morning, after
You left the photograph
The tide pools at dawn, the waves
In their black-and-white
Froth, I scavenged in your bag
For books, then picked up one
You'd thrown onto the bed, Cocteau,
Your place marked with a snapshot
Of a whale leaping clear of the spray
Tossed by the migrating
Herd—a totem
Of what you've left to dream. Yet,
It's why we've come—*Hotel Sierra*—
To this place without a past for us,
Where, I admit, a dozen years ago
I stayed a night across
The hall. I never asked why, on this
Ocean, a hotel was named for mountains
Miles inland. I spent that cold
Evening playing pinball in some dank
Arcade. Tonight, I'll take you there,
Down by the marina with no sailboats,
By the cannery's half-dozing, crippled

Piers rocking in the high tides and winds
Where I sat out on the rotted boards,
The fog barely sifting down,
The few lights
Looped over those thin, uneasy poles
Throbbing as the current came and went.
Soon, I could see only two mast lights
Blinking more and more faintly
Towards the horizon. I took
A flask of gin upstairs, just to sit
At the narrow window drinking
Until those low-slung, purposeful
Boats returned. As I
Wait here this morning, for you,
For some fragment of a final scene,
I remember how I made you touch, last
Night in the dark, those
Summer moths embossed upon the faded,
Imperial wallpaper of the room.
Now, as I watch you coming up
The brick-and-stone path to the hotel,
I can hear those loose wood shutters
Of the roof straining in the winds
As the storm closes
Over the shore. I listen as you climb
The stairs, the Nikon buzzing
Like a smoked hive
Each moment as you stop in front of:
A *stair-step; a knob of the banister;*
The worn brass "12" nailed
To our door; the ribbons: knots of paint
Peeling off the hall—
You knock open the door with one boot,
Poised, clicking off shot after

Shot as you slide into the cluttered room,
Pivoting: *me; the dull seascape hung*
Above the bed; the Bible I'd tossed
Into the sink; my hands curled on
The chair's arm; the limp spider plant . . . .
Next week, as you step out
Of the darkroom with the glossy proofs,
Those strips of tiny tableaux, the day
And we
Will have become only a few gestures
Placed out of time. But now rain
Slants beyond a black sky, the windows
Tint, opaque with reflected light;
Yet no memory is stilled, held frame
By frame, of this burlesque of you
Undressing. The odd pirouette
As your sweater comes off, at last,
Rain-soaked slacks collapsing on the floor.
Tomorrow, after we leave for good
The long story we've told of each other
So many years not a friend believes it,
After we drive along the shore to Albion
To your cabin set high above the road,
After we drag your suitcases and few boxes
up to the redwood porch,
After the list of goodbyes and refusals ends,
We'll have nothing to promise. Before I go,
You'll describe for me again those sleek
Whales you love, the way they arc elegantly
Through water or your dreams. How, like
Us, they must travel in their own time,
Drawn simply by the seasons, by their lives.

AGHA SHAHID ALI

The Keeper of the Dead Hotel

Still bitterly remembered . . . the
labor strife at the roaring copper
town of Bisbee, leading to the Bisbee
Deportation in July 1917.

In one room upstairs

                  he reads late
into the night. Afternoons wake him

to voices speaking in webs. Nights
he lights the desk lamp in the lobby,

then walks into the bar and touches
the piano.

               Drunk senators once gambled
here while their wives blurred

the balconies with silk. One,
an actress whose smile was an era,

came down the steps, turned
like the century to look at herself,

then vanished from the mirror
of the pine hatstand.

             Letters arrived
for her years after. When he reads them,

he hears her whisper: "Something
has happened. What is it?"

                No one answers,
but each night a voice cries out: "Fire!"

The copper mountains echo with rifle shots:
men on strike are being killed

in the mines, the survivors forced
into boxcars and left in the desert

without water. Their women are leaving
the city.

           Each night he sees them depart.
Each night he hears laughter from the balconies:

braceleted arms, glasses filled
with the moon's dry wine. Each night

               she still asks:
"Something has happened. What is it?"

But who will tell her? She is furiously
brushing her hair. Her shadow,

through the transom, is soft on the ceiling.
Who will tell her?

           Every silence in the world
has conspired with every other. Unanswered

she is leaving this city again, her voice
pressing him back into the silence

of ash-throated men in the desert,
of broken glasses

on the balconies,
the moon splashed everywhere.

for John Hudak

KAREN SWENSON

Surface and Structure:
Bonaventure Hotel, Los Angeles

Four black glass silos
store grains of white lights
waterfalling six levels of balconies,
outlining wired leaps
of reindeer stags that arch
the lobby pool fragrant with chlorine.
Outside, elevators, black scarabs,
crawl up the shiny walls above
pale lassoes of freeway lights.

Someday when the freeways crack up,
when the scarabs lie on their backs
in bowels of cable,
the silos, wind turning
dust devils round their bobbins,
will house kite and hawk
in their honeycombs.
Lizards flickering edges of balconies
will leave in the pool,
dry patterns of their vertebrae
exquisite as carved ivory
broken from a necklace.

In the Lobby of the Hotel del Mayo

The girl in the lobby reading a leather-bound book.
The man in the lobby using a broom.
The boy in the lobby watering plants.
The desk clerk looking at his nails.
The woman in the lobby writing a letter.
The old man in the lobby sleeping in his chair.
The fan in the lobby revolving slowly overhead.
Another hot Sunday afternoon.

Suddenly, the girl lays her finger between the pages of her book.
The man leans on his broom and looks.
The boy stops in his tracks.
The desk clerk raises his eyes and stares.
The woman quits writing.
The old man stirs and wakes up.
What is it?

Someone is running up from the harbor.
Someone who has the sun behind him.
Someone who is barechested.
Waving his arms.

It's clear something terrible has happened.
The man is running straight for the hotel.
His lips are working themselves into a scream.

Everyone in the lobby will recall their terror.
Everyone will remember this moment for the rest of their lives.

LEWIS HYDE

Hotel with Birds
  (*Mexico*)

Across the courtyard from the balcony
the pigeons walk the red clay tile
of the hotel roof, a scramble of pipes
and chimneys, flower pots, extra tile,
discarded fluorescent lights. . . .

The tiles are not fastened down.
The hot air rises through them,
the rain runs off. There is
a gutter where the pigeons sleep.

They land on the rim of the wooden water barrel
and bend over to drink, their tails
flipped up like hands raised in salutation.

They are a bird like us, with their persistent courting
and the song they mumble about the bushes of love.

I gave my heart away this winter. I had held it
in my fingers so long, heavy red clay muscle
waking me up tired in the morning.
How fine it is to have this circulation start
in another body, and come back! I am easy
on my feet, like a young girl dancing in her room,
like yesterday's sparrow that coasted through the door,
swooped 'round our room, and left without grazing a wall.

Plain brown sparrows nest in the beams
over the balcony. They hop through
the bars of the parrot's cage
and drink his water, peck at his feed.

We saw black swans in the lake at the park
bobbing their heads for each other, cooing, their song
like a wind between their bodies, not a word to be heard
just some nonsense caught in the nodes of harmony
and sent out over the dirty water and the peanut shells.

Where did I get this phrase about the heart? I just
remember Reverend Francis in his woodshop, bored,
listening to the woman complain about her son who
"hasn't given his heart to Jesus" (and Francis
nodding, rocking in his chair, leaving her alone).

Last year I'd sit by myself and read
in the barrio church. At one of the side altars
an old black-and-white etching
of the Child with an armful of hearts,
holding one forward with his left hand.
Drops of blood. The small clipped photos
of children stuck around the image
in thanks or petition. Solemn faces,
the serious mood of a photographer's booth.
Outside, a courtyard and trees painted white
at the bottom. Birds and dust.

The tiles on the hotel roof are a porous, earthy red,
like flower pots. They are just laid there without
mortar and soak up the sunlight and the heat.
The pigeons move confidently, their wiry feet clicking
as they go. They stop and coo at anything their size,
then fly up and circle, a clapping of wings, an ovation.

She took my heart as lightly as one of her own breaths,
one of her laundry hums, simple — not that
acrylic green and bossy parrot yelling *papá,*

but the dun-colored birds at the peak of the roof
where the mud tiles fold over as if melted,
where the song carries—take my heart, my purr,
my ruffled blood—and the pigeons walk,

all shoulder and breast beneath the bobbing, servant head.

In the Hotel of the Mind

RUTH STONE

The Latest Hotel Guest Walks Over Particles that Revolve in Seven Other Dimensions Controlling Latticed Space

It is an old established hotel.
She is here for two weeks.
Sitting in the room
toward the end of October,
she turns on three lamps
each with a sixty watt bulb.
The only window opens
on a dark funnel of brick and cement.
Tiny flakes of paint glitter
between the hairs on her arms.
Paint disintegrates from a ceiling
that has surely looked down on the bed beneath it
during World War Two,
the Korean War, Vietnam,
the Cuban crisis, little difficulties
with the Shah, covert action, and presently,
projected Star Wars.
In fact, within that time,
this home away from home, room 404,
probably now contains the escaped molecules,
radiation photons and particulate particles
of the hair and skin of all its former guests.
It would be a kind of queeze mixture of body fluids
and polyester fibers which if assembled,
might be sculptured into an android,
even programmed to weep and beat its head
and shout, "Which war? . . . How much?"
She feels its presence in the dim artificial light.
It is standing in the closet.
There is an obsolete rifle, a bayonet.
It is an antihero composed of all the lost neutrinos.

Its feet are bandaged with the lint of old sheets.
It is the rubbish of all the bodies who sweated here.
She hears it among her blouses and slacks
and she knows at this moment it is, at last,
counting from ten to zero.

MARTHA RHODES

In This New England Inn's Bed

I dream I'm a go-go dancer
40 like I am, but
tinselled
slippery
straddling tables
dipping my toes
into men's and women's gins
vodkas
every drink
clear and iceless

and dream I'm making love
to all the Christmas Eve guests
the cook
the room maid
her husband in his reindeer suit
and why the hell not the whole town
what's keeping *you* outside in the cold
I shout through the window
to the gas pumper across the street
thumbs in his pockets

In this bed I stuff a pillow
under my nightgown pretending
I'm twenty-eight and pregnant
and reach for a towel
draped over the Windsor rocker
and bite down hard against the pain

Romanticism

Tonight rain spills from the clogged gutters.
Say a man wakes up in the middle
of this noise, wakes up in a small room
in a hotel or a boarding house, one
of those places he has stayed in
longer than he told himself he would.
He hears the rain, and he's reminded
of some romantic vista,
then of a woman standing
on a porch, looking out, lightly
touching her hair. He tries
to remember the name of a lover from
ten years ago, but the scene
is an old postcard pasted to the glass
of a bureau, drapes frayed,
the smudged-up window looking
out on yet another building.
It passes. Let's not make him feel
too bad, or burden him
with our sorrows.
He turns over and goes back
to sleep, thinking that all of this
is what he never desired
for himself. Or he can't decide.
The rain is such evasive consolation,
spilling off the roof, just so.

GALWAY KINNELL

The Man on the Hotel Room Bed

He shifts on the bed carefully, so as
not to press through the first layer
into the second, which is permanently sore.
For him sleep means lying as still as possible
for as long as possible thinking the worst.
Nor does it help to outlast the night—
in seconds after the light comes
the inner darkness falls over everything.
He wonders if the left hand of the woman
in the print hanging in the dark above the bed,
who sits half turned away, her right hand
clutching her face, lies empty,
or does it move in the hair of a man
who dies, or perhaps died long ago
and sometimes comes and puts his head in her lap,
and then goes back and lies under a sign
in a field filled nearly up to the roots
holding down the hardly ever trampled grass
with mortals, the once-lovers. He goes over
the mathematics of lying awake all night alone
in a strange room: still the equations require
multiplication, by fear, of what is,
to the power of desire. He feels around—
no pillow next to his, no depression
in the pillow, no head in the depression.
Love is the religion that bereaves the bereft.
No doubt his mother's arms still waver up
somewhere reaching for him; and perhaps
his father's are now ready to gather him
there where peace and death dangerously mingle.
But the arms of prayer, which pressed his chest
in childhood—long ago, he himself, in the name
of truth, let them go slack. He lies facedown,
like something washed up. Out the window

first light pinks the glass hotel across
the street. In the religion of love to pray
is to pass, by a shining word, into the inner chamber
of the other. It is to ask the father and mother
to return and be forgiven. But in this religion
not everyone can pray—least of all
a man lying alone to avoid being abandoned,
who wants to die to escape the meeting with death.
The final second strikes. On the glass wall
the daylight grows so bright the man sees
the next darkness already forming inside it.

LUCIE BROCK-BROIDO

The Letter L

Someday I won't feel things anymore.
In the false light of a hotel room

Where the sheets will be old, worn
Into a perpetual softness by strangers,

A grim moon catches in the boughs
Of the old lamp by the bed,

I am your apprentice. I look for the L
In my name in places of light, lucky,

The good ending of tenderly. The psychic
Leaves the past, sand covers Egypt,

Moves constantly to arrive at the streak
Of the yet-to-be. It's quirky, this grace

Of telling, the low moonlight of an odd
Decade all over the linoleum floor.

He smells light souring
Cream, something wrong.

Near the harbor where the little lights
Will be strung up for the solstice,

When it's time, I will look there
For your name. You have taught me

To look for lies in relics,
Jewels, flaws. I come home

& someone's always in the back seat
Of my car, wailing for Ray Charles,

Left handed, one window left lit
In a small town full of dark trailers,

Late winter, last of the 1900's.
Someone is still awake.

CHARLES SIMIC

For the Sake of Amelia

Tending a cliff-hanging Grand Hotel
In a country ravaged by civil war.
My heart as its only bellhop.
My brain as its Chinese cook.

It's a run-down seaside place
With a row of gutted limousines out front,
Monkeys and fighting cocks in the great ballroom,
Potted palm trees grown wild to the ceilings.

Amelia surrounded by her beaus and fortune-tellers,
Painting her eyelashes and lips blue
In the hour of dusk with the open sea beyond,
The long empty beaches, the tide's shimmer . . .

She pleading with me to check the ledgers,
Find out if Lenin stayed here once,
Buster Keaton, Nathaniel Hawthorne,
St. Bernard of Clairvaux, who wrote on love?

A hotel in which one tangos to a silence
Which has the look of cypresses in silent films . . .
In which children confide to imaginary friends . . .
In which pages of an important letter are flying . . .

But now a buzz from the suite with mirrors.
Amelia in the nude, black cotton over her eyes.
It seems there's a fly
On the tip of her lover's Roman nose.

Night of distant guns, distant and comfortable.
I am coming with a flyswatter on a silver tray.
Ah the Turkish delights!
And the Mask of Tragedy over her pubic hair.

Inhospitable

You, too, have walked the carpeted halls
with an empty ice bucket, pretending
to look for the machine, but really listening
for passion's channel
blaring from bolted-down, pre-set tvs.

You, too, have felt the little escalator
of despair along your spine, the incessant
and just-entirely-too-damn-much
resonant expansion and contraction
along the ductwork of your ventilation system;
the frustration of being
a breeze faced with cities — continually deflected,
too easily separated, from the general windiness —
of having come so long a way
to die in alcoves and lobbies behind closing doors.

Back in your room, in a deep sea video of Antarctica,
the sunlight, dulled and flattened
by its journey through the ice pack,
suffuses grim upper layers of ocean
with a beauty capable only of
that which can take or leave us.
The divers — dark, minnow-like,
their flippers languid, their oval masks upturned —
are of no consequence.

What place has ever come to us? Beyond
the end windows of each L-shaped wing,
the volcanic city has solidified, reverted
purely to planned, utilitarian architecture
equipped with telescoping fire escapes — those
interlocking catwalks of logic, those

gangplanks of Pythagorean principle—
behind which, on the desks of offices,
pale light shines—the shade your mom
called "peaked" when writing notes
to explain your absence from school.

The Illumination

In that hotel my life
rolled in its socket
twisting my strings.
All my mistakes,
from my earliest
bedtimes,
rose against me:
the parent I denied,
the friends I failed,
the hearts I spoiled,
including at least
my own left ventricle—
a history of shame.
"Dante!" I cried
to the apparition
entering from the hall,
laureled and gaunt,
in a cone of light.
"Out of mercy you came
to be my Master
and my guide!"
To which he replied:
"I know neither the time
nor the way
nor the number on the door . . .
but this must be my room,
I was here before."
And he held up in his hand
the key,
which blinded me.

EDWARD HIRSCH

Hotel Window

Aura of absence, vertigo of non-being—
could I ever express what happened?
It was nothing, really, or next to nothing.

I was standing at the window at dusk
watching the cabs or the ghosts of cabs
lining up on the other side of the street

like yellow ferryboats waiting to cross
a great divide. All afternoon the doorman
whistled through the shadows, Charon

slamming doors and shouting orders
at traffic piling up along the curb.
People got into cars and disappeared—

ordinary people, tourists, businessmen—
while fog thickened the city's features
and emptied out the color. I don't know

how long I stood there as darkness
inhabited air itself, but suddenly,
when it happened, everything seemed dis-

jointed, charged with non-existence,
as if a vast, drowned lake was rising
invisibly—permanently—from the ground.

At the same time nothing really changed,
footsteps still echoed in the hallway
and laughter flared up the stairwell,

the passengers flinging themselves into cabs
never noticed they were setting forth
on a voyage away from their bodies.

I felt within a sickening emptiness—
intangible, unruly—and I remember
lying down on the floor of the room . . .

Then the phone rang and it was over.
Nothing happened—it took only a moment—
and it was dizzying, relentless, eternal.

Europe and Beyond

Hôtel des Grandes Écoles

The window across from the bed,
like everything else in Paris
this jet-lagged, water-logged day,
is a little crooked. On my eyelids
it is an orange rectangle that seems to float,
smaller and smaller into darkness.
Jerking in and out of sleep
I slip off the edge of a precipice
that turns out to be a ledge
just three feet off the ground.
But it takes so long to fall
I hear myself crash
like someone slamming a piano shut,
far, very far away.
All I know of Paris is the rain—
and this room with its pink-and-white wallpaper
where eighteenth-century lovers
exchange flowers and scented notes.
Even from this distance
I can hear the song
the school children of Paris
sing beneath our window.
I am confused enough to think
that I wrote it for you.
Confused enough to think
we have slipped back a few centuries—
that I hear the rattle of carriages
and horses clip-clopping over cobblestones.
I did not want to come here
because caddis flies large as thumbnails

were due to hatch at a certain lake I know.
You insisted that I see the sky over Notre Dame.
I know there is a rumor going around—
that we are an unlikely amalgam
of fire and ice under high pressure.
They say we have come to Paris
to settle a running argument about clouds.

The Enormous Aquarium
(after Proust)

All morning long from inside the lobby
Of the Grand Hotel, the empty seashore
Hung suspended there like a tapestry
Of no particular interest or value,
And it was only at intervals, while cards
Were shuffled and dealt around the fours,
That one of the players, finding nothing
To do, might turn his head to glance outside
At an occasional sail on the horizon.
And so, too, the afternoon hours, immutable
And bland, would pass before the windows
That more and more, as the sun declined,
Came to seem like mirrors in which you look
And find no other face but your own.

But then the evening arrived, the heat
Of the day settled onto the sand,
And suddenly it happened—as though
At the gesture of an imaginary hand—
That a great hidden stream of electricity
Would flood the dining rooms and halls
Until the hotel became, in its alluvial glow,
Like an enormous aquarium against whose
Glass the fishermen's and the tradesmen's
Families, clustering invisibly in the outer
Dark, would press their faces to look in.
And how like strange fishes the occupants
Now seemed as they floated past on those
Golden eddies of unrippling light: there,

A Serbian officer whose organdy plume
Was like the blow of spume off some great

Blue whale; and there, a young man who,
From his earliest years, had obviously moved
In the freshest waters of Faubourg Saint-Germain;
Or there, grand and aloof, the dowager Duchess,
Her powdered jaws closing on a morsel
Of food like a primitive shellfish closing
On a spore. . . . And the question now lingering
In the air was how the glass could sustain
A world so vastly different from the poor,
A world where tea gowns and sable, grosgrain
And crepe de Chine, topaz and silver
And the enameled ring that encircled a wrist

All spoke of a life grown infinitely
Distant and unreal. Yet if, from out
Beneath the eaves, the unwearying, gentle
Flight of the sea-martins and swallows
Had not arisen just then—one beyond another,
To shiver the air like a playing fountain,
Like dying fireworks strewn out along
The shore—without the sudden lull
Of that brief interruption, they might easily
Have stayed much later at the glass,
Instead of turning, as they did, beneath
A disc of moon as round and white as an eye,
To walk back home down the darkened streets
Like some ancient and magnificent tribe.

Section III

At the Queen's Park Hotel, with its white, high-ceilinged rooms,
I reenter my first local mirror. A skidding roach
in the porcelain basin slides from its path to Parnassus.
Every word I have written took the wrong approach.
I cannot connect these lines with the lines in my face.
The child who died in me has left his print on
the tangled bed linen, and it was his small voice
that whispered from the gargling throat of the basin.
Out on the balcony I remember how morning was:
It was like a granite corner in Piero della Francesca's
"Resurrection," the cold, sleeping foot
prickling like the small palms up by the Hilton.
On the dewy Savannah, gently revolved by their grooms,
snorting, delicate-ankled racehorses exercise,
as delicate-ankled as brown smoke from the bakeries.
Sweat darkens their sides, and dew has frosted the skins
of the big American taxis parked all night on the street.
In black asphalt alleys marked by a ribbon of sunlight,
the closed faces of shacks are touched by that phrase in Traherne:
"The corn was orient and immortal wheat,"
and the canefields of Caroni. With all summer to burn,
a breeze strolls down to the docks, and the sea begins.

DEREK WALCOTT

Section XXXVI

The oak inns creak in their joints as light declines
from the ale-colored skies of Warwickshire.
Autumn has blown the froth from the foaming orchards,
so white-haired regulars draw chairs nearer the grate
to spit on logs that crackle into leaves of fire.
But they grow deafer, not sure if what they hear
is the drone of the abbeys from matins to compline,
or the hornet's nest of a chain saw working late
on the knoll up there back of the Norman chapel.
Evening loosens the moth, the owl shifts its weight,
a fish-mouthed moon swims up from wavering elms,
but four old men are out on the garden benches,
talking of the bows they have drawn, their strings of wenches,
their coined eyes shrewdly glittering like the Thames'
estuaries. I heard their old talk carried
through cables laid across the Atlantic bed,
their gossip rustles like an apple orchard's
in my own head, and I can drop their names
like familiars—those bastard grandsires
whose maker granted them a primal pardon—
because the worm that cores the rotting apple
of the world and the hornet's chain saw cannot touch the words
of Shallow or Silence in their fading garden.

MARVIN BELL

A True Story

One afternoon in my room
in Rome,
I found, wedged
next to the wheel of a wardrobe,
so far under
no maid's broom could touch it,
a pouch made from a sock.
Inside were diamonds
in several sizes. Spread on the carpet,
they caught in my throat.
I knew that, from that moment on,
I would never answer the door.
All of my holiday
would be a preparation
for leaving. First,
I would have to leave the hotel,
probably the city.
I knew someone I could trust
and another with nerve.
She would carry home
half of them, perhaps in her underwear,
if it was not of the kind
customs officers like to touch.
I would carry the others
by way of Zurich,
stopping to purchase
eucalyptus cigarettes, chocolates
and a modest music box
with its insides exposed.
After that, who knows?
Keep them for years?
Lug them into the shade and sell cheap?

A trip to a third country?
A middleman?

So long as I didn't look up,
there with the stones before me
in the old room in the old city—
where embellishment of every fixture
and centuries of detail
took precedence
over every consideration
of light, air or space—
so long as I did not look up
to my suspicion,
I held the endless light of a fortune
and the course of a lifetime.

In retrospect, it was entirely appropriate
that my diamonds
were the ordinary pieces
of a chandelier, one string of which
had been pulled down
by a previous tenant of room three,
perhaps in a fit of ecstacy,
For I found, also—a diamond-
shaped third of its cover
hanging down from behind the wardrobe,
face to the wall—
the current issue of one of those men's
monthlies in which half-
nude women, glossy with wealth,
ooze to escape
from their lingerie.
And in the single page in its center,

someone had held his favorite
long enough to make love.
The pages were stuck together elsewhere also,
in no pattern,
and the articles on clothing and manners
left untouched.

So this was no ordinary hotel room,
or the most ordinary of all!
Men had come here many times no doubt
to make love by themselves.
But now
it was also a place of hidden treasure.
The rush of wealth and dark promise
I took from that room
I also put back. And so too everyone
who, when in Rome,
will do what the Romans do.

LOUIS SIMPSON

Out of Season

Once I stayed at the Grand Hotel
at Beaulieu, on the Mediterranean.
This was in May. A wind blew steadily
from sea to land, banging the shutters.
Now and then a tile would go sailing.

At lunch and dinner we ate fish soup
with big, heavy spoons.
Then there would be fish, then the main course.

At the next table sat an old woman
and her companion, Miss O'Shaughnessy
who was always writing letters
on the desk in the lounge provided for that purpose —
along with copies of *Punch* and *The Tatler*
and an old wind-up Victrola.

There was a businessman from Sweden
and his secretary. She had a stunning figure
on the rocks down by the sea.
She told me, "My name is Helga.
From Vasteras" . . . brushing her hair,
leaning to the right, then to the left.

Also, an Englishman who looked ill
and went for walks by himself.

    O

I remember a hotel in Kingston
where our mother used to stay
when she came on one of her visits
from America. It was called
the Manor House. There was a long veranda
outside our rooms, and peacocks on the lawn.

We played badminton and golf,
and went swimming at Myrtle Bank.

I did jigsaw puzzles, and water colors,
and read the books she had brought.

In the lounge there were newspapers
from America . . . "Gas House Gang Conquer Giants."
What I liked were the cartoons,
"The Katzenjammer Kids" and "Bringing Up Father."

◐

Getting back to Beaulieu . . .
this could have been one of the places
where the Fitzgeralds used to stay —
the bedroom thirty feet across,
a ceiling twelve feet high.
The bathroom, also, was enormous.

A voice would say . . . "Avalon,"
followed by the sound of an orchestra,
and . . . shuffling. This would continue
all night, till two or three,
when the last pair of feet went away.

I was preparing to shave
when an arm came out of the wall.
It was holding a tennis racket.
It waved it twice, moved sideways,
flew up, and vanished through the ceiling.

◐

Of course not. Yet, it's weird
how I remember the banging shutters
and the walk to the village
past cork trees and slopes lined with vines.

Narrow, cobbled streets going down to the sea . . .
There would be boats drawn up, and nets
that a fisherman was always mending.

I sat at a table overlooking the Mediterranean.
At the next table sat the Englishman
who looked unwell. I nodded.

He paid for his drink abruptly
and strode away. Terrified
that I might want his company.

○

At times like this, when I am away from home
or removed in some other way,
it is as though there were another self
that is waiting to find me alone.

Whereupon he steps forward:
"Here we are again, you and me . . .
and sounds . . . the chirping of birds
and whispering of leaves,
the sound of tires passing on the road."

Yes, and images . . . Miss O'Shaughnessy
shouting "Fish soup!" in the old woman's ear.
The businessman from Vasteras
and his girl . . . lying on her side,
the curve of her body
from head to slender feet.

The Englishman walking ahead of me . . .
He has a stick; as he walks
he slashes with it at the reeds
that are growing beside the road.

These things make an unforgettable impression,
as though there were a reason for being here,
in one place rather than another.

The Hotel

It sat under a hood of snow and pine,
a burrow rich with dens,
and we inside: mothers and children,
nuns and forty-nine orphans, in rows
of rooms like little breathing pockets.
Outside the war roared on, the whole
world at war the women said,
all its countries, all its people.
But we lived in rooms
like boxes stacked row on row.
The lights went on and off, and the corridors
stretched from one end to the other.

In bed next to my sleeping sister
I am alone in our room. My mother
turns off the light and leaves us
after we're tucked in, to sit
with her mother and her sister in a room
at the far end of the corridor
under the lamplight: three women knitting,
shadows in their laps and their words
stretched taut like threads, counting
the loops on the long needles.
Some nights I think they're counting
the rooms of my life. If I were there
under the light, they might show me
rooms like so many lanterns, lit up
and flickering with people and voices,
flickering with all I wish to do.
But they'd never show me
the room I want to know about the most,
the one that waits like a black box
and is still and incomprehensible.

The Landlady in Bangkok

Because, separated from us by a language,
we find her a character without a plot,
a cotyledon without an ecosystem,
we invent her a husband, in the alley court,
a barren womb in this quiet cell of Bangkok's hive
under trellised vines in tin cans.

We graft invention on observation,
imagine her dispossessed
by a second wife's fecundity,
while she keeps her clothes in plastic bags
and sleeps upstairs on the corridor floor
before doors of the Spartan rooms she rents us.
We pass on hypotheses with other travelers' news—
names of hotels in Burma,
prices of guides in Borneo.

We know she counts herself to sleep with our money,
yet hoards notebooks grinning
with our faces which she forgets
with our comments she can't read.
But her records like our fabrications
are errant gestures around a kind of love.

She has no picture for our words for home
as we've no history for the wheal
of scar raised on her shoulder
as at the temple stairs she
buys piping sparrows in wooden cages
and frees them to gain merit—
each a traveler fluttering
from Samsara to Nirvana.

Motel Seedy

"the room wants to be rid of me. . . ."
Denis Johnson

Motel Seedy

The artisans of this room, who designed the lamp base
(a huge red slug with a hole
where its heart should be) or chose this print
of a butterscotch sunset,
must have been abused in art class
as children, forced to fingerpaint
with a nose, or a tongue. To put this color
green—exhausted grave grass—to cinder blocks
takes an understanding of loneliness
and/or institutions that terrifies.
It would seem not smart to create
a color scheme in a motel room
that's likely to cause impotence in men
and open sores in women,
but that's what this puce bedspread
with its warty, ratty tufts could do. It complements
the towels, torn and holding awful secrets
like the sail on a life raft
loaded with blackened, half-eaten corpses . . .
I think I owned this desk once, I think
this chair is where I sat
with the Help Wanted ads spread and wobbling
before me as I looked for jobs
to lead me upward: to rooms
like this, in America, where I dreamed
I lived . . . Do I deprive tonight
the beautician and her lover,
a shower-head salesman, of this room?
He is so seldom in town.
I felt by their glance in the hallway
that my room, no. 17, means
something (don't ask me to explain this) special
to them. Maybe they fell fiercely

into each other here for the first time,
maybe there was a passion preternatural. I'm glad
this room, so ugly, has known some love
at $19.00 double occupancy—
though not tonight, for a dollar fifty less.

DENIS JOHNSON

In a Rented Room

this is a good dream, even if the falling is
no less real, and even if my feet will crumble

on the lurking ground. my throat itches, and i am
awake in this room which is no less vacant for

all my presence and there are no aspirin. here
is the sun with its tired surprise, the morning. there

are the cars and streets moving in the usual
fashion. the room wants to be rid of me. it must

fall open and communicate with other dim,
stifled rooms when i have slaughtered my body in

the sheets and fumbled streetward to soothe the itch. what
do you learn, room? what have you told, why are the stains

and the accusing glasses pointing so when i
return? there was the girl some time ago. *she* would

want to know where the guilt comes from, that hums over
the bed and descends, like an uncaring thumb, to

blot me out. she would help me, when the universe
has fooled me again, and the joke has gone too far,

when the itch, climbing, deep, remains after bottle
after bottle, and i inch toward death and i

must poke my body into a thousand vacant
darknesses before i strike the correct sleep, and dream.

At the Days End Motel

I turned on the waterworks and said
"Well you don't need to make a Federal case out of it."
But she did and I suppose she needed to.
Let's get out of this hellhole, I said.
That's a nice dog and pony show you have there, she said.
Be my guest, I said.
You're really chewing up the scenery tonight, she said.
And you, you're a predatory woman, one of easy morals, cheap
     and tawdry.
Hey listen schmendrick, at least I'm not an inept nonentity.
Aw, Cupcake, don't let's get cruel now, I can't help for stains
     on the wallpaper, okay?
You're like a rabbit responding very rapidly to food.
I confess, in a crutch and toothpick parade
     I would never single you out.

Down the road, about a quarter of a mile, a tractor trailer
     jack-knifed and took a stationwagon and a mini-bus with it
     straight to hell where they had some remarkably good
     carrot-cake.
A jackal-headed god of the underworld
     joined them at their table
     and was surprisingly convivial.

GREG PAPE

In the Bluemist Motel

I hear voices in the next room
that stop and the closing of a door
in the Bluemist Motel in Florence, Arizona,
across the road from the state penitentiary,
where I am about to close the venetian blinds
to mute the light that shines all night
from the guard towers and the sign.
In this room, I imagine, two brothers
plotted the escape of their father
who had murdered a man in a rage
but had always loved his boys.
They made it almost to Gallup
before their stolen van was stopped
at a roadblock, just north of the Río Puerco
on Defiance Plateau, and the shooting began.
One of the boys took a bullet in the brain
and died there under the stars and shattered
glass. Now, the other brother and the father
live in separate cells across the road
and listen, as I do, at intervals all night
to the metallic voice of the loudspeaker
giving instruction in numbers and code.
This is years ago as I stand at the window
with the cord in my hand dusted blue
from the neon sign that buzzes over
the parking lot and the locked cars.
I don't know why all this comes back
tonight, insistent, as if I might
have done something to change the course
of these lives. As if I might have stepped in
between the father and the man he was about
to murder and said something strong and final
so that the father turned away in shame
and the sheriff never pulled the trigger

and the boy is still walking around somewhere
with a perfectly good brain he's finally
learning how to use, and his brother
has decided to marry again for the second
or third time and, because he's put in
a good day's work and he's tired, the father
is falling asleep in his own bed.

Desert Motel before Dawn

Up at 4:00 A.M., an hour and a half
or a lifetime of darkness yet to come,
the sun just touching the waves
breaking on the Atlantic shore,
or blocked by clouds reluctant
to let the light down on avenues
already crowded with workers.
Here, others stir in the rooms, brothers,
sisters, fellow workers who, for a moment
as they try to shake off one dream
and slip into another, don't know who
or where they are. California City,
they were told, but who can be sure?
This room is familiar and anonymous,
the No Tell Motel anchored to the desert
with cement, a small idea that hardens,
and stapled into a box to keep out
most of the wind, sun, and hordes
of desert tortoises that come out
after the rains. This room among rooms
stocked with cheap beds remade each noon,
prepared by a maid from Coahuila
for the marriage of heaven and hell.

Pickups idle in the parking lot, workers
fill the big aluminum coolers
with gallons of water, the cook in the cafe
lays out the lines of bacon
and beats the eggs. A waitress downs
her coffee, lights her second cigarette,
and says here they come again Jesus to no one.
We should probably stop here
and leave them to their breakfast,
the tedious work ahead, the sorry jokes

no one needs to hear.
We could go back to the motel together
where a couple not unlike ourselves
have been up and down all night,
soldiers in the war for peace and happiness,
laborers at love working away the darkness
between them, whipping up the winds
that keep the body turning, making the sun
shine and the rains rain,
freeing the hordes and the angels
who may or may not come.

LYNN EMANUEL

Outside Room Six

Down on my knees again, on the linoleum outside room six,
I polish it with the remnant of Grandpa's union suit,
and once again dead Grandma Fry looks down on me
from Paradise and tells me from the balcony of wrath
I am girlhood's one bad line of credit.

Every older girl I know is learning how to in a car,
while here I am, eye at the keyhole, watching Raoul,
who heats my dreams with his red hair, lights up my life
with his polished brogues, groans *Jesus, Jesus.*
I am little and stare into the dark until the whole small

town of lust emerges. I stare with envy, I stare and stare.
Now they are having cocktails. The drinks are dim lagoons
beneath their paper parasols. The air is stung with orange,
with lemon, a dash of Clorox, a dash of bitters;
black square, white square goes the linoleum.

Paradise Motel

Millions were dead; everybody was innocent.
I stayed in my room. The President
Spoke of war as of a magic love potion.
My eyes were opened in astonishment.
In a mirror my face appeared to me
Like a twice-canceled postage stamp.

I lived well, but life was awful.
There were so many soldiers that day,
So many refugees crowding the roads.
Naturally, they all vanished
With a touch of the hand.
History licked the corners of its bloody mouth.

On the pay channel, a man and a woman
Were trading hungry kisses and tearing off
Each other's clothes while I looked on
With the sound off and the room dark
Except for the screen where the color
Had too much red in it, too much pink.

WILLIAM CARPENTER

At the Foxtrot Motel

It was October in Presque Isle, potato season,
and all evening at the bar of the Foxtrot Motel
we'd talked about artists and their sad lives.
The kids who worked in the potato fields were
in the next room dancing; we got lugubrious
by the fire, thinking of Marsden Hartley, how
he tried to perfect his life, how he found
a young fisherman in Nova Scotia and might have
finally known happiness, but the boy drowned
in a storm off Lunenburg. He lost and lost.
His losses made him paint more beautifully, as if
he'd squeezed the colors of those landscapes out
of tubes containing his own skin and blood.
After hours, in the parking lot, I said goodnight to the two
professors of art history. I watched young couples
drive off into the Aroostook night, each of them
looking for the right spot under the moon, though
one couple stayed right there; they reclined the seats
of their Chevy Camaro, then reclined themselves into
one seat, and when I looked up there were stars
that I had never seen, between the ordinary stars,
and stars between those, as if the universe were solid
light, with just a few patches of darkness moving
apart from themselves almost like islands, like shadows
of the drowned travelling home.
At 2 A.M. I found myself
ready for action and nothing on TV but one cable channel,
a blue movie, scrambled, only the voices clear, the bodies
broken into Kandinsky shapes, kaleidoscopic. I
wanted to see them. I knew things were coming off:
I could see clothing, I could see more and more
human skin, a breast, a penis, like fragments of
the pictures my mother found once and tore up right
before my eyes. I wanted to see them whole. I played
with the antenna coupling. I wiggled it and wiggled all

the knobs, vertical hold, horizontal hold, brilliance
and contrast. I took my shoe and struck the coupling,
then struck the socket where the cable entered the wall
of the motel. The actors were breathing faster, the man
said *tell me I'm better than anything you've had,*
tell me, and she said *yes,* the scrambled image being
all pink now, a pink tidepool of hands and nipples.
If I didn't fix it fast it would be too late, I'd
be alone in Presque Isle with nothing on the screen.
I started kicking the side of the set, first softly,
then hard, kicking to the breath rhythms of the actors,
who had stopped acting, who had forgotten their lines
and instructions and were just making love like anyone.
The color screen swirled with flushed skin and with
such lovely hair that I kicked harder, wanting to see,
wanting to witness the film's climax, which would also
be the climax of the whole Presque Isle night,
the workers parked in the picked fields with their girls,
even the art history professors and their wives, all
of them set to explode like a cut star. Finally I kicked
the knob itself, while the actress on the closed channel
murmured *hurt me, hurt me,* and I said *yes, I will,* I
kicked it solid in the center of the big screen, glass
flew everywhere, one gaseous spurt of color and of
colored sparks. The room went dark and it was dark
outside, as if there'd been a street fight in Presque Isle
and someone had hit or kicked his enemy so hard the lights
went out, not just the streetlamps, but the lights
of houses, then the stars over Aroostook County, so that
there was only space, and all of us falling through it—
the potato harvesters, the night clerk at the Foxtrot,
the couple in the movie, and, somewhere, Marsden Hartley
and his drowned sailor, dead ones and living ones finally
falling in the same direction, at the same blinding speed.

Parentheses

Indiana. Noon. A man sits on a motel bed,
　　wind blows in the tree outside his window
　　　　　in the branches, twigs and leaves,
　　　　　in the elm green shadows of the leaves.

On the walls and ceiling of the man's room,
　　the tree's shadows breathe, wave with the wind.
　　　　　He sees arms in those curves,
　　　　　waving at him, reaching for something,

and parentheses too—that open and close around
　　nothing. A shudder runs through him,
　　　　　through his shoulders and lungs,
　　　　　through his eyes and thoughts,

a shudder that makes him want to get up
　　from his bed in the Indiana motel, (where
　　　　　he's in parentheses between
　　　　　Chicago and Bloomington

between his last love and the next,
　　between selling fence wire to the last hard-
　　　　　ware store and the next, between
　　　　　motels, between hopes), get up

from his bed in the Indiana motel and
　　leave. Or close the curtains at least,
　　　　　those parentheses around a window
　　　　　he doesn't think of looking through—

and won't. Behind which there's Indiana,
　　and noon, and an elm, with wind
　　　　　blowing through every branch,
　　　　　every twig, every single waving leaf.

Holiday Inn Blues

In a dark cave called Fuzzy's
    Holiday Inn Spartanburg South Carolina
  some weird ritual being performed
       by the natives
   a sign proclaiming
'Come Dance the Fuzz Off Your Peaches!'
a country-rock group working out
 an Elvis Presley singer
    bellows at four dim couples dancing
  two of them doing rock-style
        not touching
    or looking
      at each other
   as they thrash about
   as if each were trying
      to keep his or her balance
  on some erratic highspeed treadmill
The other two couples
      wrapped around each other
    in the local bear-hug style

When the number is over
      the dejected-looking couples
   wend their way back to their tables
Two of the men in lumberjack shirts
    shovel the ladies into their seats
  and retreat to their own tables

And the primitive rites continue
    as two other locals sidle up
  and ask the same middle-age ladies to prance
as I sit there making up fantastic fictional histories
  of these two made-up ladies in fancy hair-dos &
    doubleknit pants suits

One
        I imagine
                has three grown children in Greenville
                and a fat husband who travels
She has her hair done once a week
                        by a lady barber from Asheville
            who specializes in blue hair & blue gossip
At her last blue appointment
                she learned her hubby had been
                    running around with a
                        gay hosiery salesman
                                    in Atlanta
The other lady
            has never been married but
                            for many years
        has been a receptionist
                        for an elderly dentist
    and has been rumored to have always been
            quite receptive to the dentist
                whenever he said Open Wide

The cave dance comes to an end again
        and the two ladies slump back to their seats again
        and two more worthies in plaid shirts
                press themselves upon them
            and they're caught again
                            in the bear-hug clutch
                the men hanging onto them
                    as if they were
                        absolutely starved for affection
            on a life-raft somewhere
                clinging to them like life itself
                        or their mothers
        yet they are absolute strangers

returning the ladies to their tables again
with bows and 'thankya m'ams'

The bandleader makes some banter
about 'them beautiful heffers' he seen on the dancefloors
The cave ritual goes on
as other younger couples struggle up
and grapple with each other
as the raunchy singer starts his Buddy Holly numbers
Three electric guitars with red lights on them
heat up behind him
The cave lights glow redder and redder
the couples more agitated
emitting a desperate heat
The electric fenders clash together
with showers of sparks
The drummer speeds up his freight train
The loudspeakers smoke
the whole cave rocks
the writhing couples fall to the floor
and roll upon each other
with small passionate cries
lips clinging to each other
like suction cups
We've fallen into
Dante's Inferno
burning for love
We're trapped inside
Bosch's Garden of Delights
groaning with love
We're lost
in Burroughs' loveless Soft Machine
with tongues alack
for love

110

Feeding the Ducks at the Howard Johnson Motel

I wouldn't say I was dying for it.
But he was already undressed, trousers, socks, shirt
in a heap on the floor. Now it's four in the morning and he
wants to feed the ducks. I tell him the ducks are sleeping.
The ducks are awake, though, floating
around and around on the pond
like baby icebergs. It's a wonder they don't freeze,
it's a wonder there aren't videos
in every room with ducks clouding the screens.

When I was six, my parents took me
to the Jungle Queen, family dining, with portholes
over every table. Fish swam past my nose,
dull-whiskered carp, shadowy
as X-rays. I tried to squeeze crumbs
through the glass, but now I think those fish fed
on one another. He saved bread
from dinner, and throws a piece to the biggest
duck, paddling in circles. Even the taste

of our bodies comes from so far away,
from bodies and bodies where we have washed
ourselves clean and hard as stones.
If a duck shuddered into him, it would
shatter. If my tongue blew away, I might know
what to tell him. Instead, I say, Why does the orange
bedspread look hideous when duck feet, the same
color, are beautiful? He throws again
and again, the bread sinking right

in front of their beaks.
I have been hungry so long I could
lift an empty glass to my mouth and savor the air
for hours. Each time I throw bread

I feel like a child, my arm reaching out across
the pond, pitching as hard
as it can the fat balls of dough. Only
now I am aware of their dumbness,
their duck stupidity, how

they do not even see the bread, which glows
as it falls, every crust and crumb
shining under lights of the motel. Suddenly I
think of his teeth, hard
behind his lips; how, if a duck
bit me now, my hand
would open its heart, the rich
smell of something baking rising
from my flesh.

EMILY HIESTAND

Moon Winx Motel

Tuscaloosa, Alabama 1955

The Moon Winx with its neon eyes and sly smile
was the sure sign that our road trip South was over.
Only the apron of pale, rufous pebbles from the river,
and a great-aunt's driveway buckling under Goodyear tires
meant we were closer to the Gothic radios, and yellowing
sheaves of sewing pattern tissues, and the lenses
that magnified the Word of my mother's people.
Their driveways were paved in water-worn pebbles,
a fluid pelt—acrid in heat, powdered by drifting clays,
then washed by warm rains to the colors of salmon
and salamanders. Those stones could close, as cool
and snug as pockets, around barefeet when we stood
ankle-deep in the one-time bed of the Tombigbee River.
There we made a game called Going to the Moon—
looping rubber bands on gimcrack rockets,
shooting the cellophane ships into the sky,
then craning our necks—wowed by flight.
The land we learned was the land of the Creek
(rightly, the Muscogee Alliance), and it was dotted
with indigenous Coca-cola machines,
aligned with perfect posture along shank ends
of brick motels and à la mode beauty salons.
Perhaps a poodle in the window. For our nickel,
we got the sweet brown wine of America: a formula
of solvent and caramel, the oils of naroli and coriander,
and one unknown, the still secret "7X."

WILLIAM OLSEN

The Oasis Motel

I touch you like the waves admire the weirs.
It is themselves they push out from, toward what
they are a part of, and it is transportation,
and this is why palms rustle, why the moon
drops shamelessly below the horizontal
off the Gulf of Mexico, and why you, too,

are something else, and utterly familiar.
And when I turn from comfort to a fight
picking up in the outdoor bar below,
one angel has asked another if he'd like
his face pushed in on this fantastic evening—
here at the edge of our nation the ravening void

fills with his sobbing, tearless plea for mercy,
convincing me I too have dearly suffered,
I too am equally amazed at terror's
lucidity and broachable distance.
The coward angel with a bloodied face
stumbles across new silences to his car

for everyone leaves exactly when he wants to,
and the way the coastal highway freight trucks rumble
beyond all sad reproach is just too awful,
for why else would the reading lamp enclose us,
why else would your arm be thrown across
the pillow in its unforgettable journey

all the way securely to your fingers
unless the night has nothing more nor less
to do with us than some small boatlight now
heading out from shore, and where it is
is not so far from where it was, and it
is lost to sight, and it is heading forth.

Bruce Berger

Motel Room Curtains

Light through motel room curtains
Butters alike the chair,
The desk, the TV, the Bible,
The lamp, the bed and the sleepers
Caught in the quiet mirror
Like artifacts in amber,
Mixing live fluorescence
with the bodiless combustion
Of traffic that never rests
But is only abandoned awhile
In motels brilliant with safety,
Where bulbs and wheels through the curtains
In softened animation
Press on through the dreams of sleepers
Halfway somewhere else.

The Chambermaids in the Marriott in Mid-Morning

are having a sort of coffee klatch as they clean
calling across the corridors in their rich contraltos
while luffing fresh sheets in the flickering gloom
of the turgid passionate soaps they follow from room to room.

In Atlanta they are black, young, with eloquent eyes.
In Toledo white, middle-aged, wearing nurses' shoes.
In El Paso always in motion diminutive Chicanas
gesture and lift and trill in liquid Spanish.

Behind my "Do Not Disturb" sign I go wherever they go
sorely tried by their menfolk, their husbands, lovers or sons
who have jobs or have lost them, who drink and run around,
who total their cars and are maimed, or lie idle in traction.

The funerals, weddings and births, the quarrels, the fatal gunshots
happen again and again, inventively reenacted
except that the story is framed by ads and coming attractions,
except that what takes a week in real life took only minutes.

I think how static my life is with its careful speeches and classes
and how I admire the women who daily clean up my messes,
who are never done scrubbing with Rabelaisian vigor
through the Marriott's morning soaps up and down every corridor.

W. D. SNODGRASS

Leaving the Motel

Outside, the last kids holler
Near the pool: they'll stay the night.
Pick up the towels; fold your collar
Out of sight.

Check: is the second bed
Unrumpled, as agreed?
Landlords have to think ahead
In case of need,

Too. Keep things straight: don't take
The matches, the wrong keyrings—
We've nowhere we could keep a keepsake—
Ashtrays, combs, things

That sooner or later others
Would accidentally find.
Check: take nothing of one another's
And leave behind

Your license number only,
Which they won't care to trace;
We've paid. Still, should such things get lonely,
Leave in their vase

An aspirin to preserve
Our lilacs, the wayside flowers
We've gathered and must leave to serve
A few more hours;

That's all. We can't tell when
We'll come back, can't press claims;
We would no doubt have other rooms then,
Or other names.

Dining Late

"Around us a promiscuity of settings, . . ."

Heather McHugh

The Partial Explanation

Seems like a long time
Since the waiter took my order.
Grimy little luncheonette,
The snow falling outside.

Seems like it has grown darker
Since I last heard the kitchen door
Behind my back
Since I last noticed
Anyone pass on the street.

A glass of ice water
Keeps me company
At this table I chose myself
Upon entering.

And a longing,
Incredible longing
To eavesdrop
On the conversation
Of cooks.

Cleveland Summer of Nickel Tips

In the daily pallor of tablecloths,
I served them macaroons,
ladyfingers, cherry squares,
pots of iced tea
sweating like summer colds,

and clenched my trays, steeped in heat,
pouring headlines of victorious youth
into the gaze

of ladies in stickpins and rouge,
throats full of dusk.
The sniffling ills of growing old
with not a single thank you note
as the hot Cleveland wind
blew its tune from a score of work.

One large order of Florida pie,
the temperature of love,
green the year round. I did what I could.

Marmalade at dawn, devil's food at noon,
Cleveland's reward for industry
in a haze of nickel days.

The Bus Boy

It was a smarmy restaurant, serving the tied
and jacketed, well-groomed seducers and their shills
with credit cards. Do the rich have souls? Is envy

the empire of the poor? We who shuffled to the kitchen
shoveling salmon onto china, who uncorked
chardonnay for our bosses, searched the parking lot

for open glove compartments, thought of arson
as an angel like Saint Francis, the burning fat
our stigmata, but we were just a cold carafe

of water, prelude to the bread and butter,
prelude to the rich and flaky pastry dough, that
wafer-thin desert, espresso and the check, tenor for

a dead-pan maitre d', our Napolean, our Saint Peter.

GARY HAWKINS

The Manager

Swaying through tables on tiptoes
on eggshells, on the heels of guests,
he holds his drink perfectly,
at waist height, a low level
of ice cubes, the flat, dry line of vermouth.
No matter that this liquid forms
a film in his mouth, that the dining room
seems concave to him, bowl-like,
and he's made the proper adjustments —
like the nearly blind do — to navigate
the furniture.

          He runs this place
in a cloud of his own gin, settling now
in the wide chairs of the bar, glass
in front of him before he even sits,
his Tanqueray sipped in, breathed out
and inhaled once more in a kind
of recirculation that seems to keep
the atmosphere in check, mediating
the dense air of the cooler, the kind
that can absorb the smoke from a joint
as if sucking quickly, all for itself.

Good God, this is the life. Timeless,
as the numbers on the till push together,
as the last customers straggle out,
as he fumbles with the door —
no matter that the tables start to spin,
a gasp like breathing under water and chill
like ice on the spine, a swizzle stick
pushed down to his sphincter until,
hell, this joint is on air, fans twirling
a tornado of haze, and he's beneath a barstool
to keep from falling through the ceiling's ragged hole.

KURT BROWN

Two Restaurants

1. The Trough

A place for gluttons, one big room gleaming with tile—
floor, walls, ceiling—antiseptic and brightly lit. No
romance, here. This is serious. A customer
arrives and strips. He's huge. A hill of pink fat. He's
given a plastic bib, a full smock that fits over his head
like a transparent poncho. Now he squats under a table
made of stainless steel. There's a rubber grommet in the
middle. He pokes his head up through it and a waiter
appears, dressed in a wet suit, with a shovel of spaghetti.
The customer opens his mouth and the waiter pushes the
spaghetti forward, letting the blade of the shovel slide
easily across the hard steel. Some of the food slides
over the customer's head, past his ears, around the solid
column of his neck. He's red and glossy. He stops chewing,
opens his mouth, and the waiter pushes up another load.
In the end, the customer pays his bill, takes a shower
in one of the stalls off the main room, dresses and leaves.
The waiter comes back tugging a hose. A powerful jet
of water gushes out, washes everything down a bright grille
in the center of the floor. Soon the tiles are gleaming,
the table is clean. The door opens and another large man
enters, lumbers across the room, and takes off his clothes.

2. The Glass Case

A place of orchids and marble, carpet that swallows
even the faintest echo of sound. The leaves of palm
trees glisten. A rosy light flushes the walls. Some
customers enter—a couple in their mid-thirties dressed
to the nines. They take their seats and a shimmering
glass booth settles over them, four walls and a roof,
raised and lowered by a system of pulleys hidden in the
ceiling. Air—purified, cool, rich in oxygen—seeps in
from an unknown source. The tablecloth is immaculate,

the plates and dishes glow. The silverware is silver,
the goblets gold. A waiter appears, outside, in a
form-fitted tux. He pushes a fancy cart laden with
food: succulent turkeys, platters of roast beef and
fish, desserts like jewels, all under glass lids. The
customers point, ordering dinner with vague movements
of their wrists. The waiter returns with their food
in a small transparent cabinet. He attaches this to
the side of their booth. Now the waiter shoves his
arms into a pair of shoulder-length gloves built right
into the walls. He looks like one of those technicians
in a nuclear plant handling dangerous isotopes. Using
the gloves, he opens a small door in the wall where the
box of food is attached, takes out each plate, and sets
it in front of the customers. He pours wine, sets down
a basket of bread, fluffs up the roses which stand in
a vase at the center of the table. Now he pulls his
arms back out of the gloves and wheels the cart away,
returning periodically to thrust his hands back into
them. He replenishes the wine, scrapes some crumbs
discreetly off the table with the edge of a knife and
they're sucked up. The dishes are cleared in reverse:
lifted with gloves from the table, placed in the
box attached to the wall. The door is then closed, the
box detached and carried away on the cart. A check is
brought. The waiter leaves. The customers place their
money on a silver tray, and stand up. The glass booth
lifts away from them, silently, and disappears into the
ceiling. The two of them smile. The man takes the woman's
hand and leads her out between the husky trunks of two
royal palms.

The Buckhorn Exchange

On this perfectly clear fifth of July
we're the strays, lucky ones who got away,
collecting ourselves over rare elk steaks,
collaborating like gristle and bone.
Tonight's old home week at The Buckhorn Exchange.
Nostalgia, glamour, lights, camera,
handfuls of please-take-our-order.
And who complains?
The badger's dead going on sixty years,
the fledgling quails keep their hopeful pose.
Thousands of well-preserved heads watch us
share our sparks of salt and pepper.
Someone went so far as to have stuffed
the eggs. Conversation's an upstart.
It's floating up the stairwell.
Do we want to take dessert and cordials
on the upper deck? Suspicion is at rest,
stuffed, langorous, awash, almost asleep.
Someone's hidden the Victorian settee
under layers of Oriental shawls.
Their silken fringes have tickled an idea
to death. Oh, Sympathy, you pour raggedly
into one friable vessel. We're full up
to our necks. Anyway, the scientologist
at the neighboring table won't stop bellyaching
against his detractors. He hates what we miss
on his tone scale. Zero point zero,
we're ready for our check. According to him,
if we're in luck we'll arrive effortlessly
at pain, a zone of neutral preoccupation;
perhaps we'll reach a state of conservation,

a preservation we've inhabited too often.
Thank God, the waiter's nonchalant.
Enthusiasm, eleven full steps above the grave.
He serves a giant tip.
He's from our neck of the woods.
He's authentically glad we came.
He hopes we'll come back again and again
to add a spark of life to these rooms
so empty of heartbreak and loss.

At Bickford's

You should understand that I use my body now for everything
whereas formerly I kept it away from higher regions.
My clothes are in a stack over against the orange pine cupboard
and my hair is lying in little piles on the kitchen floor.
I am finally ready for the happiness I spent my youth arguing and
    fighting against.
    Twenty years ago—walking on Broadway—
I crashed into Shaddai and his eagles.
My great specialty was darkness then
and radiant sexual energy.
Now when light drips on me I walk around without tears.
—Before long I am going to live again on four dollars a day
in the little blocks between 96th and 116th.
I am going to follow the thin line of obedience
between George's Restaurant and Salter's Books.
There is just so much feeling left in me for my old ghost
and I will spend it all in one last outburst of charity.
I will give him money; I will listen to his poems;
I will pity his marriage.
—After that I will drift off again to Bickford's
and spend my life in the cracked cups and the corn muffins.
I will lose half my hatred
at the round tables
and let any beliefs that want to overtake me.
On lucky afternoons the sun will break through the thick glass
and rest like a hand on my forehead.
I will sit and read in my chair;
I will wave from my window.

JOAN ALESHIRE

The Man from the Restaurant

The man watching her house is indistinguishable
from the doorway opposite until he steps out,
shakes his head in surprise at the rain
that's begun to fall, and walks a few paces
down the street. The woman recognizes
the back of his head which she sees
every day but Sunday bent over his menu
at lunch. Quiet, he settles in his chair
as if it's his only comfort in a hard world.
The way he asks what she recommends, chooses
that, his thanks, make her think of him
on evenings like this one, when her lover
hasn't called, when her early hopefulness
has bled like color from the rainy sky.

Now the man comes back, stands so still,
so like the sculptured stone side of the doorway
she begins to be afraid—not that he's
a rapist or even a voyeur. His upturned face
shines in the streetlight, intent, hopeful
as a child's. How can she fail
to disappoint him? By now, she feels
she can't answer any man's questions, except
maybe the simple ones: her boyfriend's
"Can I come over?" at midnight; or "Buy you
a beer?" from the bartender at work when she
leans into her own reflection, polishing tables
at the end of a long afternoon, leans as if
hoping to find someone younger, full of ambition,
in the vague shape that shines back.

RAYMOND CARVER

Reading Something in the Restaurant

This morning I remembered the young man
with his book, reading at a table
by the window last night. Reading
amidst the coming and going of dishes
and voices. Now and then he looked
up and passed his finger across
his lips, as if pondering something,
or quieting the thoughts inside
his mind, the going
and coming inside his mind. Then
he lowered his head and went back
to reading. That memory
gets into my head this morning
with the memory of
the girl who entered the restaurant
that time long ago and stood shaking her hair.
Then sat down across from me
without taking her coat off.
I put down whatever book it was
I was reading, and she at once
started to tell me there was
not a snowball's chance in hell
this thing was going to fly.
She knew it. Then I came around
to knowing it. But it was
hard. This morning, my sweet,
you ask me what's new
in the world. But my concentration
is shot. At the table next
to ours a man laughs and laughs
and shakes his head at what
another fellow is telling him.
But what was that young man reading?
Where did that woman go?
I've lost my place. Tell me what it is
you wanted to know.

PHYLLIS KOESTENBAUM

Admission of Failure

The hostess seats a girl and a young man in a short-sleeve sport shirt with one arm missing below the shoulder. I'm at the next table with my husband and son, Andy's Barbecue Restaurant, an early evening in July, chewing a boneless rib eye, gulping a dark beer ordered from the cocktail waitress, a nervous woman almost over the hill, whose high heel sandals click back and forth from the bar to the dining room joined to the bar by an open arch. A tall heavy cook in white hat is brushing sauce on the chicken and spareribs rotating slowly on a squeaking spit. Baked potatoes heat on the oven floor. The young man is eating salad with his one hand. He and his girl are on a date. He has a forties' movie face, early Van Johnson before the motorcycle accident scarred his forehead. He lost the arm recently. Hard as it is, it could be worse. I would even exchange places with him if I could. *I want to exchange places with the young armless man in the barbecue restaurant.* He would sit at my table and I would sit at his. After dinner I would go in his car and he would go in mine. I would live in his house and work at his job and he would live in my house and do what I do. I would be him dressing and undressing and he would be me dressing and undressing. Our bill comes. My husband leaves the tip on the tray; we take toothpicks and mints and walk through the dark workingmen's bar out to the parking lot still lit by the sky though the streetlights have come on as they do automatically at the same time each night. We drive our son, home for the summer, back to his job at the bookstore. As old Italians and Jews say of sons from five to fifty, he's a good boy. I have worked on this paragraph for more than two years.

LAWRENCE FERLINGHETTI

Ristorante Vittoria, Milan

Three baldheaded men at the next table
　　speaking accented English which is
　　native to none of them
Maybe two are Italian and one is from
　　Egypt and doesn't know the *bella lingua*
They are discussing deepsea mining
　　(One thousand meters down—nodules!)
Perhaps I should report it to the CIA
　　(that international terrorist group)
Suspicious discussion in American
　　the language of the conquerors—
We are alone in the restaurant
　　among the linen-covered tables
　　and the huge silver
I decide at length that they are all Italian
　　putting me on
　　for some perverse reason
I decide to pretend I don't understand
　　the strange language they are talking
　　maintaining an inscrutable and urbane countenance
　　like some debonair expatriot character
　　in Henry James
　　putting my meat in my mouth
　　with the fork in the left hand
　　in the Continental manner
　　having read an international spy novel
　　in which the American fugitive
　　gives himself away
　　by changing his fork back to his right hand
　　before raising it to his mouth
I am seriously pursuing this line of behavior
　　as the three men with bald nodules
　　continue their seemingly serious discussion
　　about the deep sea

off the coast of Abyssinia
though at any moment we might all
burst out in riotous laughter
at the ludicrous absurdity
of the whole charade

MICHAEL PETTIT

Vanna White's Bread Pudding

If not famous ourselves, oh let us
nudge up against stars and starlets

everybody knows, everybody envies
for all the sweet attention they receive.

Like when in Mother's Restaurant
a table opened up for us, lucky guys,

next to the table in the corner
where three good-looking women sat,

attended by some sharp fellow
and looks from all the other patrons.

Damn if we didn't set down our gumbo
and red beans and cold Dixie beer

beside the TV personalities in town
to do business and enjoy good food.

Damn if it wasn't Vanna White herself
sitting there, in the flesh, in pink,

face from the Wheel of Fortune weeknights,
figure that turned the letters round

and turned all the heads in Mother's
and drew a chorus of whispers—

Vanna White, Vanna White, Vanna White
next to us, not an arm's length away.

And when the owner himself came over
insisting she try the famous bread pudding—

despite her protests, despite her trim waist,
despite the waste she hated to see—

damn if Vanna didn't turn, smiling,
and offer her bread pudding to me. To me!

Damn if I didn't say thanks, and take it.
Damn if it wasn't sweet, buttery, hot,

and therefore gone in a wink, like a star falling
into my heretofore but no more anonymous lap.

Mr. Ho's

*Either it doesn't help
or it isn't needed.*
        FORTUNE COOKIE

Cheers from Mr. Ho, who can't stand
simplicity, who each year adds
more gaudy New Year's bunting, more
tinsel and froufrou to his ceiling
and walls and tables. I take a seat
and he's on me, hustling his Fogcutters,
his Navy Grog, offering me everything
in the bartender's fat book.
I have a No thank you for each,
a No please for all the appetizers,
a No for the veil Ho's Chinese bellydancer
flounces across my neck as I wait for
my sweet and sour pork. Can't they see
I am here for simple Chinese fare
and not to cure some melancholy?
Perhaps the drunk across the room
needed his last flaming drink
and it may have helped to tuck
his dollar next to the bellydancer's
creamy skin, to hear her ululations
and watch her ass shimmy away
in her gauzy pantaloons. It seems so:
now he's smiling and Ho is smiling
and she is smiling, looming over me
with her perfume and sweat, hot
for a tip. But it is my neck,
my night to hang my head and goddamn
if I want this, want anything
but my pork, stale cookie and the check.

PETER SEARS

The Tablecloth Explanation

It's all because the round man with the pumpkin neck
was teaching no one in particular macadam composition,
and because a lady giggled like dry fire when the

bartender who liked lighting his lighter and looking
at it said a fellow wanted to be a vampire to get
the inside story but he had bad knees from football,

so he talked ladies into sponsoring a blood bank
and they all lounged in the blood bank lobby in
cracked leather chairs and sweep-around sunglasses,

gurgling, snoozing, bloated as ticks. Meanwhile,
I was sharpening my fork under the table,
under my napkin, humming over the ominous grating,

figuring one turn in the air maybe two, depending,
depending on the balance of the fork.
Thud a couple in the walls about ear high,

to keep them at bay, but they charged me with chairs
and water pitcher grenades and tied me up in these
tableclothes. I was badly outnumbered officer.

STEPHEN DOBYNS

Tenderly

It's not a fancy restaurant, nor is it
a dump and it's packed this Saturday night
when suddenly a man leaps onto his tabletop,
whips out his prick and begins sawing at it

with a butter knife. I can't stand it
anymore! he shouts. The waiters grab him
before he draws blood and hustle him
out the back. Soon the other diners return

to their fillets and slices of duck. How
peculiar, each, in some fashion, articulates.
Consider how the world implants a picture
in our brains. Maybe thirty people watched

this nut attack his member with a dull knife
and for each, forever after, the image pops up
a thousand times. I once saw the oddest thing—
how often does each announce this fact?

In the distant future, several at death's door
once more recollect this guy hacking at himself
and die shaking their heads. So they are linked
as a family is linked—through a single portrait.

The man's wobbly perch on the white tablecloth,
his open pants and strangled red chunk of flesh
become for each a symbol of having had precisely
enough, of slipping over the edge, of being whipped

about the chops by the finicky world, and of reacting
with a rash mutiny against the tyranny of desire.
As for the lunatic who was tossed out the back
and left to rethink his case among the trash cans,

who knows what happened to him? A short life,
most likely, additional humiliation and defeat.
But the thirty patrons wish him well. They all
have burdens to shoulder in this world and whenever

one feels the strap begin to slip, he or she thinks
of the nut dancing with his dick on the tabletop
and trudges on. At least life has spared me this,
they think. And one—a retired banker—represents

the rest when he hopes against hope that the lunatic
is parked on a topless foreign beach with a beauty
clasped in his loving arms, breathing heavily, Oh,
darling, touch me there, tenderly, one more time!

Lunch in Hell

"I haven't eaten flesh," he said, and I
could hear him roll some rectitude across
his tongue, "for weeks now." *Flesh* is what you call
meat the first six months you don't eat any.

I nod and re-nod, then change the subject
as quickly as I can. I tell the one
about the horse who comes into a bar:
the bartender wants to know, "Why the long face?"

We talked about such things before we died.
We hadn't thought anyone was listening.
Since this is hell, nobody serves him meat.
Since this is hell, I get my words to eat.

All my cheap quips and easy lines are fanned
across my plate like panels of duck breast,
then napped with a tart sauce of rancid charm.
The menu at *Tavola Diavolo*

never changes. In fact they don't have one.
We have a regular table, the same
waiter. He greets us. He says (I confess
I miss the question mark), "The usual."

ALISON HAWTHORNE DEMING

Saturday, J.'s Oyster Bar

Hearing there's no lemon pie,
the businessman orders more oysters
cracking nautical jokes—*There will be liberty,
but not boats*—his gestures formal
as the crest on his blazer.

The waitress, buying the proprietor's
idea of provocative, wears black pantyhose
and burgundy short-shorts. She's never heard
of sherry, so she brings me something
sweet and red as I settle into the notebook

to add to my letter of this morning.
I'm not like you, celebrating marriage
with goat cheese and basil, red tulips
and champagne. On Saturday I go out alone
looking for the city to dish out

its bucket of steamers, shells
the color of rain that stipples the alley
where pleasure boats tip at their moorings
exaggerating the pitch of the storm. I pry open

the shells, swish the clams in broth
and love the near hour it takes me
to work through the tin. *Sierra Club*
it reads when I get to the bottom,
as if I'd just hiked up the Panther Trail

past knee-high yellow trumpet flowers
that out-blare the bees to camp at the summit,
look out on houses each corralled by its lawn,
where white smoke lifts from two chimneys
five miles apart, gunshots rise from the gravelpit.

Inside those houses women set tables
with linen, crystal and pears,
while I look in from the woods, think
theirs is the wilderness that can't be tamed.

for Suzanne Levine

WENDY WILDER LARSEN

Lunch with My Ex

I know he will order
two spritzers and rice pudding
if it's on the menu
and that his mother's name will come up.

Everything else is different
It would be easier to touch
the waiter's hands than his
which once touched me all over.

I can see how we fit together
like two continents.

Now looking at him
is like looking at a map
seeing in pastel colors
only the names of places
I knew and loved.

I hear him talking.
Near the plate is a white piece of paper.
"A quit claim to your part
of the Vermont land. That's all.
Why are you staring?"

I pick at my food remembering how
for fifteen years the phoebes came back
every spring to our house
to nest under the window frame.

How we called to each other like children
"The phoebes are back. The phoebes are back"
and they called *phoebe phoebe*
their dark tails dipping with each cry.

CHARLIE SMITH

Redneck Riviera

We ate at a poor restaurant
that was brightly lit and where the waitress
who was new at the job
tried hard to get our orders right
and brought a piece of streaky fish
that was tough and tasteless while around us
sunburned families from country towns in Alabama
and south Georgia ate the same food
without saying much
to the waitress or each other.
It was such a starry night
and we were such a long way from home,
still so shaky with each other
after the scare of our marriage falling
apart, that I leaned over and kissed
you on the mouth and tasted the lemon
and the dry baked fish
like ashes on the lips of the dead.

ELIZABETH CLAMAN

La Terrasse des Marronniers

We sit in the sudden rain, my hands spilling over.
Your hair gone slick, you look like a seal.
The umbrella is stuck. You give up, laughing.
I sit across from you, mildly amused.
How can you? I ask, dodge the question again?
I want to cry; who would notice here?

The waiter runs through the rain,
spilling tea on wet gravel.
He takes our money. Points to
inside. The others watch us.
How the rain sheets the terrace.
My hair turning dark.
How the leaves swirl down.
We sit on out here anyway
and you say, *Men are different.*

But it's not commitment,
I tell you, and slip off
this ring. You laugh. *Not again.*
But the waiter runs back.
He offers a towel, and says, *Please. Please.*
I shake my head. Sip the tea growing cold.
It makes me want to scream, you say.
Or laugh. Or cry.
The waiter shrugs, tray over his head.

You're holding me hostage, I say.
This joining at the hips like freaks.
This seasonal urge.
I drop the ring in my cup.
Will the tea lick it clean?
The storm gusts down twigs.
(A quaver of voices from inside the café.
What are they doing out there?)

I shake back my hair, and close my eyes.
We won't live forever, you say.
We won't. I wipe my hands on the white wet cloth,
then drink down the tea, ring and all.

I'm sick of this game, I tell you.
I imagine the ring gliding down, dense pink tissue.
This time I'm warning you. Next time too late.
But you jump as high as I when the thunder rolls
and the café windows reverberate.

HEATHER MCHUGH

The Most

The dining room is empty at the country inn.
We are, for your comfort, far from the town
of your friends, of mates and mistresses, and of
amends. The maitre d', whose only prey
we are, brings pickles, beans in vinegar
and switches on the musical not even he
(left to his own devices) would have listened to.
My face is in the cup of my hands.
You consider it.

Around us a promiscuity of settings,
vainness of display—like mockeries of our
intentions, linens stretch untouched and white
as far as I can see. The fish will be

untender when it comes, but I won't have
the heart to say so; we will find ourselves
in other rooms, you wondering repeatedly
how long my husband works. For now we make

the most of our opposing faces. Waiters
come and go, you settle on a suitable
entree, the room grows huge, the afternoon
appears, a glaring error, waste
of windows. "What I hate,"
you say, "is public places."
I look around and see
uninterrupted emptiness.
The wine glass fills with sun,
a slow bright bomb. The mob in me sits still.

Spilled

The waiter dropped a tray of glassware and
the din of conversation stopped as if
in shock at competition. Not
until that moment were we
quite aware

of what a roar
the ordinary made—not till a knife of
other noise could cut right through it
to the greater emptiness, to zero, there

where no one for a moment
said a blessed word. And then
the nothings started
coming back, the hum
of small talk re-arising
gradually to flow and
circulate again, its rhythms
welling up out of the hole in the story
to make the story normal once again,
the cruise control back on,
the life as a career
in which we can afford,
as usual, to fail to hear.

O

This restaurant's a dressing up of selves
in dreamy twos and fours. Their fantasies
are being fed, their livings made.
These hundred couples can, tonight, pretend

they are accustomed to such cooks and maids and then,
by some consensual agreement (because none

can really be the monarch of the model) must ignore
the commonplace proximities, the many

foreign monarchies that eat their fill
nearby. We make do with
a little privacy, say three by two, and make
believe we're different. The dream is purchased

at the price
of never seeing being
from above, or from a distance, somewhere
difference might disappear. And all

of what is being said, in this packed room, and all the other
rooms on earth, might add up to a single animal's
identifying cry—flung far
on waves of ether, waves

of ESP. For all we know
that's how a God is reached, in whose
bright synaesthesias of sympathy a blood
need not be red, if spilled as speech . . .

Dining Late

There are no burnt croutons in the restaurants of Heaven.
No overindulgence of manna will put on weight.
Reservations are eternally held between seven
And half past eight.

Most manifold are manna's manifestations:
Chicken cacciatore, beef bordelaise,
Pilafs, quenelles, marinades, decoctions, confections
And forever unfallen soufflés . . .

No margerine, microwaves, maîtres chilly or nervous,
Mis-added checks or after-effects to the wine
Will elude a Management that allows neither service
Nor fare to suffer decline.

And after denouncing glazed waiters, seats behind posts,
Pepper mills, calamari greasily fried—
Ascending to take her place with the bounteous hosts,
Seated just to the side

At the flawless table she'd met her deadlines craving,
Adoringly slicing lamb with a silver knife,
with her heavenly Escort sits the food critic, having
The time of her afterlife.

Goodbye Hello in the East Village

Three tables down from Allen Ginsberg we sit
in JJ's Russian Restaurant. My old friend,
who's struggled for happiness, insists
on knowing why I'm happy. An end
to my troubles of the century? *"Listen Molly, if I
didn't know you so well, I'd think you were
faking this good cheer,"* she says, her eyes
bright openings like a husky's eyes in its fur.
(My friend is half an orphan. It's cold in here.)
The East Village shuffles past JJ's window,
and we hear Allen order loudly in the ear
of the waitress, *"Steamed only! No cholesterol!"*
"I could tell you it's my marriage, Nita,
and how much I love my new life in two countries,
but the real reason," I beam irresistibly at a
dog walker with 8 dogs on leashes in the freezing
evening outside JJ's window where we sit,
"is that I'm *an orphan*. It's *over*. They're
both dead." Her lids narrow her eyes to a slit
of half-recognition. "I couldn't say this,"—there!
the waitress plunks two bowls of brilliant magenta
borscht, pierogi, and hunks of challah
—"to just *anybody*,"—jewel heaps of food on Formica
—only to you, who wouldn't censure me,
since you've witnessed me actually fantasize
chopping their heads from their necks from their limbs
to make a soup of the now dead Them to feed
the newly happily alive Me.

                       An old order is dimmed,
just as now the U.S., its old enemy
the USSR vaporized, disarms itself,
nearly wondering what a century's fuss
was all about . . . what *was* my fuss about? (The wealth

of relief after decades of distrust,
makes you wonder why you did it, until
you remind yourself of how it was.)
But even a struggle to the death is levelled
in the afterlife of relief. A bevel
in the glass of America has connected
along a strip of this life to the window
of JJ's restaurant connecting Nita and me, wed
to the nightlife on Second Avenue, though
in reflection only, the reflection that now perfectly
joins Ginsberg with his steamed vegetables
and us with our steamy borscht and pierogi
to the ice-pocked sidewalk, God's table,
full of passersby, pointing occasionally to Allen,
joined now by an Asian boy, but more often
just hurrying past in the cold as we eat
the food of a previous enemy
and find it brightly delicious — *it is meet
and right so to do* — in the world now ours,
the century's hours hurtling behind
like snow-wake off an empty dogsled.
Old friends, we rest, not talking, well fed,
since at this cold dark moment things are fine.

The Seven Doors

The waiter carries a white towel over
his left arm; when the couple enters
he bows his head before leading them
to a corner table. They ask for menus,
so he bows again. Instead he brings
a flagon of such dark red wine
it appears black in the candlelight
as he pours it, first into her glass,
then into his and goes off in silence.
There are seven ornate doors leading
into the large room, but no one leaves,
so the new couples that enter must
stand by the solemn doors waiting
as the candles burn slowly down, so
slowly it appears that moment by moment
nothing has changed. Nothing has changed.
One hundred years ago Gustavo Muntaner
borrowed a modest fortune at low interest
from his father-in-law and founded
The Seven Doors using his daughters
as collateral. Ships sailed from distant
ports bringing saffron, bananas, tea.
Later sealed trucks ground up the heights
where they executed the small businessmen
and their clerks in 1936, one bullet
for each as a new dawn bloomed upon
the perfect bay. Then there was peace,
the dark night of decades of utter peace.
This long day's last light breaks through
the high leaded windows, staining some
couples red, some blue, some nothing
at all. The menus arrive. The waiter

stands at attention, humming a song
not even he can hear. The candles blink
on and off playing their silly games
with darkness. The kitchen fires up.
Now we can smile. Everyone eats tonight.

GERALD STERN

There Is Wind, There Are Matches

A thousand times I have sat in restaurant windows,
through mopping after mopping, letting the ammonia clear
my brain and the music from the kitchens
ruin my heart. I have sat there hiding
my feelings from my neighbors, blowing smoke
carefully into the ceiling, or after I gave
that up, smiling over my empty plate
like a tired wolf. Today I am sitting again
at the long marble table at Horn and Hardart's,
drinking my coffee and eating my burnt scrapple.
This is the last place left and everyone here
knows it; if the lights were turned down, if the
heat were turned off, if the banging of dishes stopped,
we would all go on, at least for a while, but then
we would drift off one by one toward Locust or Pine.
—I feel this place is like a birch forest
about to go; there is wind, there are matches, there is snow,
and it has been dark and dry for hundreds of years.
I look at the chandelier waving in the glass
and the sticky sugar and the wet spoon.
I take my handkerchief out for the sake of the seven
years we spent in Philadelphia and the
steps we sat on and the tiny patches of lawn.
I believe now more than I ever did before
in my first poems and more and more I feel
that nothing was wasted, that the freezing nights
were not a waste, that the long dull walks and
the boredom, and the secret pity, were
not a waste. I leave the paper sitting,
front page up, beside the cold coffee,
on top of the sugar, on top of the wet spoon,
on top of the grease. I was born for one thing,
and I can leave this place without bitterness
and start my walk down Broad Street past the churches

and the tiny parking lots and the thrift stores.
There was enough justice, and there was enough wisdom,
although it would take the rest of my life—the next
two hundred years—to understand and explain it;
and there was enough time and there was enough affection
even if I did tear my tongue
begging the world for one more empty room
and one more window with clean glass
to let the light in on my last frenzy.
—I do the crow walking clumsily over his meat,
I do the child sitting for his dessert,
I do the poet asleep at his table,
waiting for the sun to light up his forehead.
I suddenly remember every ruined life,
every betrayal, every desolation,
as I walk past Tasker toward the city of Baltimore,
banging my pencil on the iron fences,
whistling Bach and Muczynski through the closed blinds.

Hamburger Heaven

"to be among these quiet strangers . . ."

JON LAVIERI

JIM DANIELS

Short-order Cook

An average joe comes in
and orders thirty cheeseburgers and thirty fries.

I wait for him to pay before I start cooking.
He pays.
He ain't no average joe.

The grill is just big enough for ten rows of three.
I slap the burgers down
throw two buckets of fries in the deep frier
and they pop pop spit spit . . .
psss . . .
The counter girls laugh.
I concentrate.
It is the crucial point—
they are ready for the cheese:
my fingers shake as I tear off slices
toss them on the burgers/fries done/dump/
refill buckets/burgers ready/flip into buns/
beat that melting cheese/wrap burgers in plastic/
into paper bags/fries done/dump/fill thirty bags/
bring them to the counter/wipe sweat on sleeve
and smile at the counter girls.
I puff my chest out and bellow:
"Thirty cheeseburgers, thirty fries!"
They look at me funny.
I grab a handful of ice, toss it in my mouth
do a little dance and walk back to the grill.
Pressure, responsibility, success,
thirty cheeseburgers, thirty fries.

COLETTE INEZ

Short Order Cook, Blue Mill Diner

She slams down burgers
on a grill six nights a week
on the turnpike's edge,

lumbers home to a boarding house
on puffed feet, one flight up,
sharing the toilet and corridors.

Her nagging worry an only son
who lives a night away
and shatters the quiet of Monday

huffing behind two paper bags
bulging with gin.
The door distills their quarreling

to hiccups in the hall.
She hears his curses climb
down the steps of ten o'clock,

out into sozzled air, trees, night.
Up again to dredge specials
with breadcrumbs and flour,

she pounds the turnpike's edge,
her greasy hours rounding out
the passageway to Monday next.

Hamburger Heaven

A man orders a hamburger
but before he can eat it

he falls off his stool
foaming at the mouth . . .

What is it they tell you
to do with their tongue?

No one, not one customer
in all of Hamburger Heaven

has the foggiest notion.
So maybe the best thing

is to just move over—
give the guy some room.

But this guy is bleeding.
His face is turning blue.

He needs somebody strong
to force open his mouth.

He needs something to bite on
before he breaks his teeth.

His pants are wet. His head
keeps banging on the floor—

on the dumb-fuck cement
of Things-As-They-Are

until finally the loose
feckless white flag

of his Nike flies off
and it's over. Outside

in the slush somewhere
a Salvation Army Santa

rings a faint, faint bell—
but it tastes like blood.

His pants are wet. Then
a blond, ethereal waitress

hands him a shoe—enormous
in his slow comprehension

and heavy as death. Now
he can try to remember

why it was he was born
and the reason for hell

not to mention his name
or the secret of tongues

or what it was exactly
he'd specifically ordered.

LISA LEWIS

The Accident

I had no business there in the first place—
I'm putting on weight—but the counter help was all smiles,
Having survived the lunch hour crunch. My husband and I
Ordered burgers and fries; I was in front, so I chose
A seat on the far side, back to the window.
I picked off two thin rings of onion; the fries were limp.
We were talking about some recent trouble,
Something about the car, maybe, both of us
Interested, me a little bitchy, so it was almost the way you turn
Instinctively, say from a spider web in a darkened hall,
How I looked across the restaurant and found her face,
Left cheekbone swollen to a baseball, the same eye blackened,
Heavy make-up, front tooth out in a jack-o-lantern grin
As she tried to look friendly to the young waitress
Her husband motioned over. He rested one hand
On his wife's shoulder, solicitous, the other waving
A lit cigarette, a small man, dark-haired, now laughing aloud,
Glancing at the uncombed head of his beaten wife again
Turning her back to the room, though not crowded,
All suddenly staring, reading the last few hours
Of those lives in a horror of recognition.
She cupped her hand shading the side of her face,
You could see lumps of vertebrae through her t-shirt,
And he kept on talking, smiling at her, with a slight tilt
Of his head, as if saying *poor baby, something happened to her,*
Good thing I'm here to take care of her, a car wreck,
A bad one, a smash-up, and all of us looked
And knew better. At the table with them was a little girl.
The man, the woman, the five-year-old daughter—
Even the man and the beaten woman had the same features,
As people do who have lived together for years. I couldn't see
The child's face. He was jotting a note on a small pad,
The waitress's name, as if to write a letter praising
Her fine service, and she smiled through her horror, she

Hardly more than sixteen, with clear pale skin. Next to us
A woman in permed hair and suit rose to leave, lunch untouched,
With her daughter. She carried a leather legal-size folder.
We left soon after, heads turned, not looking,
Because sometime the man and woman would go
Home to the privacy of a city apartment, no neighbors
Home all day to hear, but first I said, in the restaurant,
Across the room where he couldn't hear, *If I had a gun
I'd blow his brains out*, and I thought of that moment
Familiar from movies, the round black hole in the forehead
Opening, the back of the skull blowing out frame by frame
Like a baseball smashing a window, but no one near
Would've even been bloodied because no one was standing anywhere
Near him, his hand on the beaten woman's shoulder
Might as well've been yards from his body.

I was taught not to write about this. But my teacher,
A man with a reputation who hoped I would make
Good, never knew that I, too, have been hit in the face by a man.
He knew only my clumsy efforts to cast what happened
Into "characters," and he loved beauty in poetry.
Maybe what I had written was awkward. Maybe my teacher
Guessed what happened and forbade me writing it
For some good reason, he cared for me, or he feared
He too might've slapped my face, because I, like the character
In that first effort, was bitching to the heavens and a redneck
Boyfriend, and we argued outdoors, near a stack of light wood
Used to kindle the stove like everyone has
In the foothills of North Carolina. That day I railed
Like a caricature of a bitching redneck woman,
Hands on hips, sometimes a clenched fist, I was
Bitching, I think, as he planned some stupid thing
I hated, like fishing, pitching horseshoes, driving

To visit his mother on Sundays, her tiny house
Tangled in dirt roads, where she sat in the kitchen dipping snuff.
Whatever he wanted to do was harmless,
But so was my shrieking, my furious pleading, an endless loop
Inside my head rolling *I want to be rid of him*, and he slapped me
Across my open mouth, I felt myself shut up and staggered,
Because he was a large man, and I was a large woman,
He had to make sure he hit me pretty hard,
Both of us strong and mad as hell, early
One Saturday morning, when he wanted to do what he wanted to do
And I wanted to keep him from it. He slapped me
Twice, open-handed, knocking me, open-handed, to my knees
In kindling, so my knees were scraped bloody and my hand
Closed on a foot and a half of inch-thick pine, and I stumbled up,
Swinging, my eyes popping wide, till I brought it down
Hard across his shoulder, I saw how the rage on his face
Flashed to fear, just that quick, a second, or less,
And he turned to run but he made the wrong choice,
If he'd gone to the road I wouldn't've followed, but he ran
Inside my "duplex" apartment, an old country house
Cut in two. So I cornered him upstairs and knocked him out.
It was simple. He fell so hard, I thought *I've killed him*;
I was throwing my clothes in a paper bag when I heard him
Sobbing. In the bathroom mirror I found the black eye and
    lop-sided lip,
And it seemed as if I might still take it back, the last ten minutes,
The chase, the beating, the high-pitched screaming,
The stubborn need to go fishing. But the make-up I disdained
In those years — I had just turned twenty — didn't do much
To cover the bruises. His face was clear. The knot on his head
Stopped swelling under ice. It was easy to tell him
To get the hell out and only regret it every other minute
Since there were no children, no marriage, even,

And I was young and believed I had proven
I was strong. I had beaten a man to his knees.
Months later I would go to college and stay safely there for years,
Not letting on to anyone the terrible thing I'd done, until I wrote
That clumsy poem with the unbelievable characters, and now I've tried
To do it again, this time with different characters, I've defied
My teacher, who meant for me to learn to write well,
Who meant for the world to think well of me,
And I am not sorry. If he asked why I would say
I had to do it, and that lie would be like the lie of living
Without telling, till one day seeing the beaten face,
What scared me most, the missing tooth, the tangled hair, the
    vertebrae,
The daughter. There is no use thinking what it means
About me to say this: I am not sorry. I might have killed
That man. I might have blown his brains out.

Travellers

In the coffee shops and restaurants,
the airport terminals and lounges,
the lovers are debating
the pleasures of presence versus
the pleasures of absence,

drawing diagrams and dotted lines
in the wet glassrings left behind
by other customers,
building little barricades and highways
out of breakfast crumbs.

And if, looking up, they find that they've arrived
at no conclusions,
who can blame them?
—considering the mileage on certain parts
of the vocabulary,

considering they've been stranded
once or twice before
upon the road between desire
and its destination—like a car
that's out of gas,

or a noun without an adjective.
Still they want so much
to mash their faces
into the mushy sky of something warm
and human; want to make some sweeping declarations
about the rest of their existence;
want to flap their arms

and swear that they can fly.
No jury would convict them

of anything but being hungry
for proof of their existence,

anything but the bigamy of marrying
their favorite mistake
one time or two too many.

So he draws a line of water on formica,
like a car following a highway
between A and C. She rubs a circle
in a splash of tea
like the circle you might clear

in the breath-fogged window of a speeding train.
He shreds a napkin into triangle-shaped bits;
she pierces them with toothpicks,
and together they have fashioned
the small white flags of their surrender,

the truce with fear
that lets them move a little farther out
into the foreign country
of the future
where all of us are strangers.

DORIANNE LAUX

Landrum's Diner, Reno

We slouch, half-asleep on Christmas Day,
in a domed metal diner with seven red stools.
Three lone men drink coffee, glass shakers
of salt, pepper and sugar between them,
a pyramid of creamers. A young family
orders breakfast. They taste
from each other's plates as the sun
leaks through the windows, spilling onto
their heads, their hands, like butter.
After seven years, we have begun
to love each other, to trust
the small favors, the daily gifts.
Not that there isn't passion: the hotel bed
left a mess, bright wrappers and ribbons
scattered across the floor. But we love
where we've come to, this drowsy morning
among strangers, slumped shoulder to shoulder,
holding each other up. Our round and clumsy
waitress owns the place, trundles
between the counters filling cup after cup.
When she walks the short length of the diner,
each floorboard aches under her weight, shakes
us awake. She stops before us and lowers
her face, unlined, moon-shaped,
between our faces, her hands outstretched
palms up, in love with her work, asking
what more we could want?

The Husbands

I watch the New England Foliage bus tour stop
in Bar Harbor, and they are all old women, who
descend from the bus to the Acadia Diner, talking
about lobster salad and about their husbands, who
were pilots, lawyers, distributors of fine meats,
but are now deceased. They take over the Acadia.
They leave a space between each seat and order
two meals apiece, as if their tour guide had been
starving them. I wonder who will occupy those seats,
who will eat those extra lobsters, when a door
opens and the husbands appear, one after another,
out of the men's room, fastening their clothes,
looking at their hands and feet as if they were
seeing them for the first time. The wives tell them
about their children and their children's children;
but the husbands only want to learn what cars
they drive, what cars their children drive. They
stare into the street, hoping a Studebaker will
drive past, a new DeSoto, a Hudson Hornet, but
their wives force them to eat, thinking if they eat
they will become physical again, they will return
to beds so empty that the women spend their lives
on buses: the Covered Bridge tour, the Grand Circuit
of the Finger Lakes. After they eat, after the bus
carries the women back to their motel, the husbands
play poker and cribbage late into the night, talking
about the War, for they were all soldiers, and they
pull up their trouser legs to show their wounds, some
mortal, some superficial. One of the husbands finds
a set of antlers and dances among the tables, for
they are happy to be together, and as the horned man
dances, they sing about the seasons passing, about
enormous pheasants and women with grey fur like wolves.
In the motel, the wives hear snow brushing the windows;

they smell something like dry snow as their husbands
enter and undress. All their married lives, they were
afraid at just this moment, but it now seems natural
to have another body in the bed, to have familiar hands
finding their waists and breasts, finding their hearts,
which skip and speed up like the small hearts of girls
watching their first movie, when a star appears
for whom they would do anything, if he were only real
and sitting beside them in the dark. They feel a draft,
as if a door had been left open, so they move closer
to their husbands, thinking of how it was, how it would
be if they could only have new bodies and could feel
what they feel now, seeing the faces of their husbands
in the light of the *no vacancy* sign beyond the window
as the snow drifts around the bus, burying its wheels,
its windshield, so that the tour will not be going
anywhere tomorrow, and they can sleep forever.

A Woman

There's nobody here
but you, sitting under
the window at the corner
table as if waiting
for somebody to speak,
over your left shoulder the moon,
behind your head a vagina,
in pencil, emblazoned
above a telephone number.
For two hours you've been
looking across the street,
quite hard, at the grand store,
the Shopper's Holiday felled
across the sunset.
It grows dark in this climate
swiftly: the night
is as sudden and vacuous
as the paper sack the attendant
balloons open with a shake
of his scarred wrist,
and in the orange parking
lot's blaze of sulphur
arc lamps, each fist
of tissue paper is distinct,
all cellophane edged
with a fiery light that seems
the white heat of permanence
and worth; of reality;
at this hour, and in this
climate where how swiftly
the dark grows, and the time comes.

C. K. WILLIAMS

The Regulars

In the Colonial Luncheonette on Sixth Street they know everything there
is to know, the shits.
San Terminadi will tell you how to gamble yourself at age sixty from
accountant to bookie,
and Sam Finkel will tell you more than anyone cares to hear how to
parlay an ulcer into a pension
so you can sit here drinking this shit coffee and eating these overfried
shit eggs
while you explain that the reasons the people across the street are going
to go bust
in the toy store they're redoing the old fish market into—the father and
son plastering,
putting up shelves, scraping the floors; the mother laboring over the
white paint,
even the daughter coming from school to mop the century of scales and
splatter from the cellar—
are both simple and complex because Sam T can tell you the answer to
anything in the world
in one word and Sam F prefaces all his I-told-you-so's with "You don't
understand, it's complex."
"It's simple," Sam T says, "where around here is anyone going to get
money for toys?" The end.
Never mind the neighborhood's changing so fast that the new houses
at the end of the block
are selling for twice what the whole block would have five years ago,
that's not the point.
Business shits, right? Besides, the family—what's that they're eating?—
are wrong, right?
Not totally wrong, what are they, Arabs or something? but still, wrong
enough, that's sure.
"And where do they live?" Sam F asks. "Sure as shit their last dime's
in the lease and shit sure
they'll end up living in back of the store like gypsies, guaranteed: didn't
I tell you or not

when the Minskys were still here that they'd bug out first chance they
      got, and did they or no?"
Everyone thought the Minsky brothers would finally get driven out of
      their auto repair shop
by zoning or by having their tools stolen so many times, Once, Frank
      Minsky would growl,
on Yom Kippur, for crying out loud, but no, at the end, they just sold,
      they'd worked fifty years,
And Shit, Frank said, that's fucking enough, we're going to Miami, what
      do you want from me?
But Sam F still holds it against them, to cave in like that, the buggers,
      bastards, shits . . .
What he really means, Sam, Sam, is that everyone misses the Minskys'
      back room, where they'd head,
come dusk, the old boys, and there'd be the bottle of schnapps and the
      tits from *Playboy*
in the grimy half-dark with the good stink of three lifetimes of grease
      and sweat and bitching,
and how good that would be, back then, oh, how far back was then?
      Last year, is that all?
"They got no class: shit, a toy store," Sam T says. What does that mean,
      Sam? What class?
No class, that's all, simple: six months there and boom, they'll have a
      fire, guaranteed.
Poor Sam, whether the last fire, at the only butcher store for blocks the
      A&P hadn't swallowed,
was arson for insurance as Sam proved the next day, or whether, the
      way the firemen saw it,
it was just a bum keeping warm in the alley, Sam's decided to take it
      out on the strangers,
glaring at them over there in their store of dreams, their damned pain-
      in-the-ass toy store.
What's the matter with you, are you crazy? is what the father finally
      storms in with one afternoon,

both Sams turning their backs, back to their shit burgers, but old Bernie
     himself is working today,
and *Hey,* Bernie says, *Don't mind them, they're just old shits, sit down,*
     I'll buy you a coffee.
Who the fuck do they think they are? Here have a donut, don't worry,
     they'll be all right,
and of course they will be. "In a month you won't get them out of your
     hair," says Bernie,
and he's right again, old Bernie, before you know it Sam T has got me
     cornered in the street.
"What is it, for Christ's sake, Sam? Let me go." "No, wait up, it's a
     computer for kids."
"Sam, please, I'm in a hurry." "No, hold on, just a second, look, it's
     simple."

ALAN DUGAN

To a Red-Headed Do-Good Waitress

Every morning I went to her charity and learned
to face the music of her white smile so well
that it infected my black teeth as I escaped,
and those who saw me smiled too and went in
the White Castle, where she is the inviolable lady.

There cripples must be bright, and starvers noble:
no tears, no stomach-cries, but pain made art
to move her powerful red pity toward philanthropy.
So I must wear my objectively stinking poverty
like a millionaire clown's rags and sing, "Oh I

got plenty o' nuttin'," as if I made
a hundred grand a year like Gershwin, while
I get a breakfast every day from her for two
weeks and nothing else but truth: she has
a policeman and a wrong sonnet in fifteen lines.

Waitress

There is a table in the back where she opens
her mouth to red lipstick, lets her eyes down
for a touch of blue mascara, and rests

her bunioned feet. Six more hours
before she can sip Coca-Cola and sleep
in front of her father's new Magnavox 14 inch Black & White,

Milton Berle running across the screen.
She touched Mr. Berle's hand once in 1948
when he raised his right arm for her

and a roast beef sandwich. The world shrieked,
rang in promise. She knows it was then the twitching began
in her left eye. Esther is still

waiting tables at Dubrows. Sadie still hanging coats
at Sutters. Sunday, she's got her cousin Lenny's
green Chevrolet. The tall kitchen doors swing back

and forth, parting the hair on her forehead.
She can taste the salt at the back of her throat
thinking of the man

who will lean into her one night. Not the girl
smiling, balancing three bowls of soup on her left arm,
but a woman who would claim all beauty hers,

not to keep it, but to hold it long enough to change.

Summer Storm

The waitress props open her book
against the sugar bowl
but doesn't read it.
She hums along with the hard rock station,
a song about a brittle love
and a piece of someone's heart.

Like a face behind the drawn shade
it had nothing to do with him.
She pours his coffee,
she will do that much.

He stares at his hands,
the coffee cup, the door,
saying nothing. She is beautiful.
When she shakes out her hair
he thinks of water spilling out
or the last moonlight shaking itself
out of the trees.

Could that be thunder
in the distance
or just the music rattling
in his ears? Anyway
he's stopped listening,
even to the radio.

Even the weather station
means nothing to him now.
He knows to sit still
and wait for thunder.
He's got time on his hands.
A good rain is worth a hundred years.

She stares out the plate glass windows.
Pinpoints of light
from the next town are blinking on.
He'll look at her now and then,
but not all of her,
a sleeve, a breast,
a glimpse of hair,
long like the longest night.

Her legs are thick and muscular,
any tree on the side of the road
he could climb. He imagines himself
lost in the leaves
like the pages of some amazing book
and not one word between them.

Can a man ever make a woman
understand the weight of his own voice
lying on his chest? A love like that
takes years, means nothing
to the girl counting out-of-state plates
out in the parking lot, keeping time

to the wailing guitars
climbing up towards the roof
where a hard rain is beginning to fall.
He could nail his house
to a music like that.

But this is not a song.
This is not a love story,
and anyway, who would tell it?
Here in the deep libraries of lost causes.
A girl working her way through college.
A farmer dreaming up a tree.

JON LAVIERI

The Beacon of Winchester County

As if the night has opened
its one, bleary eye, that light
goes on in the diner.
Every now and then the town black and white
coasts by, watching and yawning.
Nothing keeps time but the wax and wane
of the stainless steel coffee urns,
bolted to the wall like models
for skyscrapers of the future.
You know the couple working
that sleepy narrow line have been there
since they were childhood sweethearts.
Now they move around each other perfectly,
as if touching broke the plates.
The two sitting next to each other,
staring at their faces in the coffee,
were married once, to other people
probably still in Winchester somewhere.
I am here for now. My back to the window,
fifteen cents for a twenty cent coffee.
Too late to be passing through
but to be among these quiet strangers
who care even less about talking to me
as I to them as we pour our faces into our cups.

Meditation on Lloyd's Diner

Lloyd's old parking lot
is a choppy sea of gravel,
rutted from back hoe tires
as if unthinkable pythons spent long
uneasy nights there.
It will be a parking lot again
once the new building is up.
Now it is a nondescript cube of cinder block
with long, dark windows.
The sign still reads "Lloyd's"
with its arrow pointing to the new structure.
I imagine this one
will have alarms sensitive to body heat,
and from where the wreckers
tore out the long formica tongue
of counter will be a glass barrier
between you and the face you see.
Not the same face that looked
so pasty but warm under fluorescent light
in a nursely white uniform
with a rectangular plastic pin that says "Julie"
who approached you and your
guilty bloodshot eyes
and spilled warmth in the space between your hands.

RODNEY JONES

On the Bearing of Waitresses

Always I thought they suffered, the way they huffed
through the Benzedrine light of waffle houses,
hustling trays of omelettes, gossiping by the grill,
or pruning passes like the too prodigal buds of roses,
and I imagined each come home to a trailer court,
the yard of bricked-in violets, the younger sister
pregnant and petulant at her manicure, the mother
with her white Bible, the father sullen in his corner.
Wasn't that the code they telegraphed in smirks?
And wasn't this disgrace, to be public and obliged,
observed like germs or despots about to be debunked?
Unlikely brides, apostles in the gospel of stereotypes,
their future was out there beyond the parked trucks,
between the beer joints and the sexless church,
the images we'd learned from hayseed troubadours—
perfume, grease, and the rending of polarizing loves.
But here in the men's place, they preserved a faint
decorum of women and, when they had shuffled past us,
settled in that realm where the brain approximates
names and rounds off the figures under uniforms.
Not to be honored or despised, but to walk as spies would,
with almost alien poise in the imperium of our disregard,
to go on steadily, even on the night of the miscarriage,
to glide, quick smile, at the periphery of appetite.
And always I had seen them listening, as time brought
and sent them, hovering and pivoting as the late
orders turned strange, *blue garden, brown wave*. Spit
in the salad, wet socks wrung into soup, and this happened.
One Sunday morning in a truckstop in Bristol, Virginia,
a rouged and pancaked half-Filipino waitress
with hair dyed the color of puffed wheat and mulberries
singled me out of the crowd of would-be bikers
and drunken husbands guzzling coffee to sober up
in time to cart their disgusted wives and children

down the long street to the First Methodist Church.
Because I had a face she trusted, she had me wait
that last tatter of unlawful night that hung there
and hung there like some cast-off underthing
caught on the spikes of a cemetery's wrought-iron fence.
And what I had waited for was no charm of flesh,
not the hard seasoning of luck, or work, or desire,
but all morning, in the sericea by the filthy city lake,
I suffered her frightened lie, how she was wanted
in Washington by the CIA, in Vegas by the FBI—
while time shook us like locks that would not break.
And I did not speak, though she kept pausing to look
back across one shoulder, as though she were needed
in the trees, but waxing her slow paragraphs into
chapters, filling the air with her glamour and her shame.

MAURA STANTON

The All-Night Waitress

for Gail Fischer

To tell the truth, I really *am*
a balloon, I'm only rubber, shapeless,
smelly on the inside . . .
I'm growing almost invisible.
Even the truckers admire my fine
indistinctiveness, shoving their fat hands
through my heart as they cry,
"Hey, baby! You're really weird!"
Two things may happen: if the gas
explodes at the grill some night,
I'll burst through the greasy ceiling
into black, high air,
a white something children point at
from the bathroom window at 3 A.M.
Or I'll simply deflate.
Sweeping up, the day shift will find
a blob of white substance
under my uniform by the door.
"Look," they'll say, "what a strange
unnatural egg, who wants to touch it?"
Actually, I wonder how I'd
really like being locked into orbit
around the earth, watching
blue, shifting land forever—
Or how it would feel to disappear
unaccountable in the arms of some welder
who might burst into tears
& keep my rubbery guts inside his lunch box
to caress on breaks, to sing to . . .
Still it would mean escape
into a snail's consciousness, that muscular
foot which glides a steep shell
over a rocky landscape, recording passage
on a brain so small how could it hurt?

LYNDA HULL

Night Waitress

Reflected in the plate glass, the pies
look like clouds drifting off my shoulder.
I'm telling myself my face has character,
not beauty. It's my mother's Slavic face.
She washed the floor on hands and knees
below the Black Madonna, praying
to her god of sorrows and visions
who's not here tonight when I lay out the plates,
small planets, the cups and moons of saucers.
At this hour the men all look
as if they'd never had mothers.
They do not see me. I bring the cups.
I bring the silver. There's the man
who leans over the jukebox nightly
pressing the combinations
of numbers. I would not stop him
if he touched me, but it's only songs
of risky love he leans into. The cook sings
with the jukebox, a moan and sizzle
into the grill. On his forehead
a tattooed cross furrows,
diminished when he frowns. He sings words
dragged up from the bottom of his lungs.
I want a song that rolls
through the night like a big Cadillac
past factories to the refineries
squatting on the bay, round and shiny
as the coffee urn warming my palm.
Sometimes when coffee cruises my mind
visiting the most remote way stations,
I think of my room as a calm arrival
each book and lamp in its place. The calendar
on my wall predicts no disaster
only another white square waiting

to be filled like the desire that fills
jail cells, the old arrest
that makes me stare out the window or want
to try every bar down the street.
When I walk out of here in the morning
my mouth is bitter with sleeplessness.
Men surge to the factories and I'm too tired
to look. Fingers grip lunch box handles,
belt buckles gleam, wind riffles my uniform
and it's not romantic when the sun unlids
the end of the avenue. I'm fading
in the morning's insinuations
collecting in the crevices of buildings,
in wrinkles, in every fault
of this frail machinery.

MARKHAM JOHNSON

The All-Night Diner

Tonight, you will not tire
of waitresses with free refills.
The eggs you ordered a decade ago
may never appear. It doesn't matter.
In the next booth, James Dean
punches the jukebox on the wall,
and whispers in your ear, "no one returns
from the all-night diner,"
and you believe him.
The selection is endless,
and eternity begins with "Teen Angel,"
then "Dead Man's Curve." In back,
a medley of sunburned tourists,
just off the boat to paradise,
select Don Ho melodies
and piña coladas, or coffee
with miniature cows for cream.
Patience is not a virtue here,
but a way of watching
the waitresses in their slow
unhurried gate. They have been here
since the beginning and know
just how to walk without
bumping the stools,
or even lying down to sleep
on marbled counters, or wondering
when the pale moon will finally
rise off the front glass
to take its place in the neon firmament,
as someone pulls the shades ⋅
and turns over the vacancy sign to full.

DENIS JOHNSON

All-Night Diners

At another table, some South Americans are singing,

> *Detectives are moving across my sight.*
> *I am without humility tonight.*
> *What is my fate, what is my fate, what is my fate?*

> *We're not in this disreputable hotel:*
> *The disreputable hotels are in us,*
> *And we inhabit a hole in the light.*
> *What is my fate, what is my fate, what is my fate?*

Their countries are being torn apart,
and yet some of them may be here for the chess tournament.
Oh yes, the world is sick of itself, sitting in its car,

but after the awful rejection I suffered by you
it was night.
A chilly wind was taking
small sticks and the like down the block
and worrying the signs. The street I walked was lifeless
but for three or four silent
figures moving in their white judo suits
toward The Center for Martial Arts . . .

        O

Think of the flayed visage of our era,
the assassinated fathers, the naked hooks of
glances and the slithering
insinuations of our music,
and all our friends who have travelled so far to meet
their anagammaglobulinaemic, jail,
monsoon, AK-47 fates
in ways and places that sound
French—*laceration,*

heroin, Khe Sanh . . .
Later I was nearly killed
by a firetruck coming around a corner
filled with men completely decked out for fighting blazes.
There wasn't any siren. There was a radio playing
In the jungle
The mighty jungle
The lion sleeps tonight

and they were all singing along, a dozen
ghosts
on a ghostly ship, steering
God knows where, what kind of fire —

○

I'm trying to explain how these islands of meaningless joy
or the loss of someone close to me, like you,
can make the tragedy of a whole age insignificant.

The local priest has swept the cross from his wall
and hung a large print of Edward Hopper's
Nighthawks, wherein the figures stall
as if somebody has told a joke
the three of them have just finished laughing at
or made one of those comments that says it all
for the moment. But the guy with his back
turned to you isn't laughing. He's got some
losing proposition, got it as palpably as the tall
redhead has her matchbook, or the soda jerk
his generous monopoly on the warm
coffee and the light,

so that you have to come back to yourself in the dark
street where that proposition lives, where nothing shows

but a vague cash register in one of the windows,
and all the way home
flowers look out of their vases at you
while aspirins dissolve amid the flowers.
And beyond them, beyond the faces of their houses all
got up for a masque,

they're sleeping two by two,
igniting the rooms
with their breaths and sighs,
holding one another closer,
tears on their pillows that this life
can be shared but not this survival.

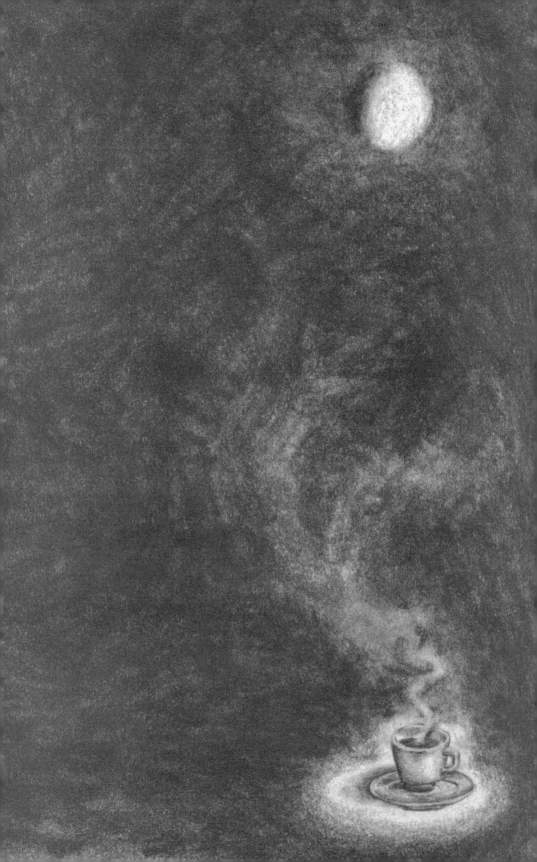

Elysian Fields

"I can recreate
This paradise anytime I choose."

Laura Mullen

CARLEN ARNETT

Morning at the Café du Monde

There is an endlessness here
at the Cafe of the World.
Tourists come in stonewashed jeans,
and shopping bags,
with maps of the Quarter, appetites
and money. The hacks sleep zigzag
on the back seats of their mist-covered carriages.

I am in New Orleans where the plaster
cannot hold without dark horsehair
worked into its swirling, elaborate fantails.
Coffee, strong, yields
to the addition of steamy milk,
and cypress floors built for use
not beauty, find their own luster anyway,
and outlast the Spanish,
the French, a war of excuses.

The women at tables around me
have mouths full
of French and expression,
and a pay phone rings back
wanting more.

CHARLES BAXTER

Fleetwood Café

The sickening lunchtime sun is pale as bouillon
in the school-of-Hopper *Fleetwood Café*,

and the sky, fated to be faded blue,
is blue, but without one reason for being itself.

This hometown sky knows all your faults by heart.
A girl dressed like a clerk drinks soup and coffee

from dishes from the five-and-dime. Her hair
is starchy and hangs away. The counterman

with apron does have a face, but the sky
has robbed it of expression, like a face

(as Europeans say) that machines would build,
childish machines. No one recognizes anyone,

or gazes at the glaring light, turned on
overhead, against all sense. The special

today is Cincinnati chili, fifty cents a bowl,
and the third person, a customer, is eating it

even though his hat's still on, giving the scene
that unpleasant dollhouse feeling,

of painted ships reduced to postage stamps. Outside,
no one on the sidewalk, or sitting in the Pontiac,

or in the barbershop with its empty chairs
and pole, a hollow wooden peppermint.

C. K. WILLIAMS

Second Persons: Café de L'Abbaye

Without quite knowing it, you sit looking for your past or future in the
    couples strolling by,
the solitaries stalking by, saddened that you never seem to find what you've
    been looking for
although you've no idea or at least you tell yourself you don't what you
    might be looking for,
you only have the vaguest, vagrant sense that it would be someone you
    knew once, lover, friend,
and lost, let drift away, not out of your life, for they were meant to drift
    away that way,
but from some portion of your meaning to yourself, or from the place such
    meaning should reside:
the other would recuperate essences, would be the link from where you
    were to where you would be,
if consciousness were able, finally, to hold all of this together, even not
    quite ever knowing why.

CAROL FROST

Patience

Café des Artistes, New York

The man raises his eyes from the table and gazes at the murals of
    women
and can tell by the styling of their hair how long ago they were
    painted—
beautifully, seductively for the roomfuls of diners to come afterwards.
So close, large in their pastel dresses, weren't they meant to be
    listening
to what one might say to a companion, who takes a swallow of cool
    wine as the man speaks,
and the waiter, full of tact, comes forward with the bottle precisely
    then, then withdraws.
How often they have felt the shapes that yearning and farewell take,
    the same few shapes.
After the table is set with precious ware, and sometimes strange—a
    marrow spoon,
a bowl of pepper (for intensities)—the guests arrive. . . ,
and the long, slow meal ends. How exposed their speeches and
    gestures.
How patient and unchanged the onlookers.

Museum Garden Café

Even from this side of the glass the way
He folds back down on itself the paper
He's been motioning with, gets up before her,
Pushes in his chair and—sort of—wanders away
Says it all. In the attention she pays
To her purse, getting up to follow him,
Looking down, being careful to fasten a clasp,
Something not quite catching, I know
It must be over; it's so formal and even
If she joins him, so they're standing side by side
Near the tall brass sculpture and she tentatively
Puts, for a moment, her hand into one
Of the nervous, complex, geometrically textured
Holes (that wound or merely interrupt?) the polished
Surface reflecting them back, in the conversation
I make up for them it's completely through.
It's spring. They're nothing to me. Beneath the bare
Poplars a mock (it will never bear fruit) plum
Has already put out its papery fragile bloom.
When they walk out the gate hand in hand
They're gone completely. I can recreate
This paradise anytime I choose.

LAWRENCE FERLINGHETTI

Café Notre Dame

A sort of sexual trauma
has this couple in its thrall
He is holding both her hands
in both his hands
She is kissing his hands
They are looking
in each other's eyes
Up close
She has a fur coat
made of a hundred running rabbits
He
is wearing a formal
dark coat and dove grey trousers
Now they are inspecting the palms
of each other's hands
as if they were maps of Paris
or of the world
as if they were looking for the Metro
that would take them together
through subterranean ways
through the 'stations of desire'
to love's final terminals
at the ports of the city of light
It is a terminal case
But they are losing themselves
in the crisscrossing lines
of their intertwined palms
their head-lines and their heart-lines
their fate-lines and life-lines
illegibly entangled
in the *mons veneris*
of their passion

Kim Addonizio

Intimacy

The woman in the café is making my cappuccino—dark eyes, dyed
    red hair,
sleeveless black turtleneck—used to be lovers with the man I'm
    seeing now.
She doesn't know this; we're strangers, but still I can't glance at her
casually, as I used to, before I knew. She stands at the machine,
    sinking the nozzle
into a froth of milk, staring at nothing—I don't know what she's
    thinking.
For all I know she might be remembering my lover, remembering
    whatever happened
between them—he's never told me, except to say that it wasn't
    important, and then
he changed the subject quickly, too quickly now that I think about it;
    might he,
after all, have been lying, didn't an expression of pain cross his face
    for just
an instant—? I can't be sure. And really it was nothing, I tell myself;
there's no reason for me to feel awkward standing here, or complicitous,
as though there's something significant between us.
She could be thinking of anything; why, now, do I have the sudden
    suspicion
that she knows, that she feels me studying her, trying to imagine
    them together?—
her lipstick's dark red, darker than her hair—trying to see him kissing
    her, turning her over in bed
the way he likes to have me. I wonder if maybe
there were things about her he preferred, things he misses now that
    we're together;
sometimes, when he and I are making love, there are moments
I'm overwhelmed by sadness, and though I'm there with him I can't
    help thinking
of my ex-husband's hands, which I especially loved, or of how dark
    he was

compared to this man's pale skin, and I want to go back to that old
    intimacy
which felt, for most of the time we were married, like the purest
    happiness
I'd ever known, or would. But all that's over; and besides, weren't
    there other lovers
who left no trace? When I see them now, I can barely remember
what they looked like undressed, or how it felt to have them
inside me. So what is it I feel as she pours the black espresso into
    the milk,
and pushes the cup toward me, and I give her the money,
and our eyes meet for just a second, and our fingers touch?

IRA SADOFF

At the Half Note Café

for Gene Ammons

Once I heard him play
"Willow Weep for Me"
in a tone so full
and sentimental, I felt
a gap between my ribs
and lungs, a dearth of air
sorrow soon enough would fill.
I found the blues unfair
to boys like me who came to bars
unprepared for grief
that wasn't strictly personal.

I told my girl
I knew all you had to know
about suffering and love, but when
I heard a woman drunk, cry out,
in front of everyone, "Don't go, Jug—
I'll give you all of what you want,"
my face went blank
and limp as an infant
when a stranger shakes
a rattle in his face. Later,
when he hit bottom,
the last broken chorus
of "Body and Soul," I collapsed in
my girl's arms, my composure crushed
by one note on the saxophone.
I couldn't think of what to tell her.
What the hell did she know anyhow?
We both came from the same suburban town.

It was a brittle winter night.
We had nowhere to go

except her parents' house,
so we drifted down Greenwich Ave.
hand in hand. I'd never seen
streets so crowded after dark—
with drunks, half-dead, and kids
who should have been in bed.
I'm shocked we made it out alive.
I know if I'd seen my stupid grin,
my wide-eyed stare, my gaping face,
I would have smashed it
just for the experience. We were lucky
though we didn't know it then. We ended up
parking in my mother's car. We kissed,
then I stripped off her blouse,
grabbed her breast,
put her stiffened nipple in my mouth.

ELIZABETH CLAMAN

Café Macondo

Sixteenth near Mission, my favorite café.
Standing in line, what a morning for memories:
In the Still of the Night, the original version
filling the coffee thick air,
and me, back in high school, slow dancing
heat through summer clothes
with some boy whose name I've forgotten.

Behind me, a man sighs, more like a groan,
and says, *God, but I was a debonnaire devil*
when this song came out. I laugh and turn,
surprised by all his broken veins, his shock of white hair.
He leans toward me and says, *Where I grew up*
there was a man lived to a hundred and seven.
And was he full of stories. Did you know Pacifica
was a breeding ground for Grizzly bears?

I shake my head, plod forward in line. He laughs.
At twenty-nine they called me the Pennzoil Poet.
Smooth as a hot butter dish, he says.
And rhythm? His eyes go foggy then close.
If you combined the clackityclack of a train
with the scatting of Ella and the way
a hummingbird's wings hold flight . . . ?
The woman in front of me wraps her hands around the cup
that holds her morning fuel, raises it sacramentally to her lips.

Next! the woman at the counter yells, her spiked hair lavender,
her green fingernails arching over the cash register keys.
I order double latte, heavy on the foam.
Listen, the Poet tells me. *Listen:*
I was the WD-40 and the snare drum,

the linseed oil and the gallop of a horse's hooves.
I laugh with pleasure. Pay for my drink. Breathe in its darkness.
He leans in close. *If you don't believe me,* he says. *If you don't believe
me—you can call up any woman in Half Moon Bay, Guadalajara, New
Orleans, Tacoma . . .*

I wouldn't dream of it, I tell him. The song ends.
The woman at the counter waves her nails like cilia.
You ready to order? The man nods, still back in time.
I was a goddamn Grizzly Bear, he tells her. *Down at the foot of Market
so thick with grizzlies men went out only armed, in packs . . .*
She glares at him. *Espresso. Double.*
He calls out after me as I walk to my table, *Highwire staccato
and the tongue of an anteater . . .*

FREDERICK SEIDEL

Pressed Duck

Caneton à la presse at the now extinct Café Chauveron.
Chauveron himself cooking, fussed
And approved
Behind Elaine, whose party it was;
Whose own restaurant would be famous soon.

Poised and hard, but dreaming and innocent—
Like the last Romanovs—spring buds at thirty, at thirty-two,
We were green as grapes,
A cluster of February birthdays,
All "Elaine's" regulars.

Donald, Elaine's then-partner,
His then-wife, a lovely girl; Johnny
Greco, Richardson, Elaine, my former wife, myself:
With one exception, born within a few days and years
Of one another.

Not too long before thirty had been old,
But we were young—still slender, with one exception,
Heads and necks delicate
As a sea horse,
Elegant and guileless

Above our English clothes
And Cartier watches, which ten years later shopgirls
And Bloomingdale's fairies would wear,
And the people who pronounce chic *chick*.
Chauveron cut

The wine-red meat off the carcasses.
His duck press was the only one in New York.
He stirred brandy into the blood
While we watched. Elaine said, "Why do we need anybody else?
We're the world."

ALISON HAWTHORNE DEMING

Caffe Trieste

American experience . . . so often is grief disguised as plenitude.
W. S. DI PIERO

It's too hot for April and the recycled Hawaiian shirts
for sale on Grant Street cost fifty bucks.
I hate the way the past gets turned into marketing—
the fifties now chrome walls fanning over formica,
polished until they look as if no one ever ate a cracker there,

and the waitresses wearing caps shaped like take-out french fry
    containers.
They're not the fifties when bombs spread like bacteria on culture
    plates,
when the cost of a family staying together might be Stelazine and
high-voltage erasures. They're just American—all shine and no pain.

Grant Street—a crowd spills out of the Caffe Trieste,
accordion music and a woman singing arias that make bystanders weep.
It's not just her singing, says one who's stood long in the sidewalk's heat.
It's the way she delivers—a swaggering Carmen slapping down
the empty wineglass in a boast, the way she shakes her head

at the close of the high note as if coming up from a muscular dive.
Then the man who stands with a portable mike near the door,
not particularly well-dressed or theatrical, but charming,
cuts an aisle through the tables, setting her up for the harmony
the audience wants to feel, announcing—*My daughter*—more
    surprised

than the bystanders who walked past vintage shops, windows
dressed with roped-up salami and the new formalism of pasta,
to find that these sounds could come from anyone's body—much less
bone of my bone—songs of passion and cruelty
reaching in to a place that wants to let loose.

PHILIP LEVINE

The Midget

In this café Durruti,
the unnamable, plotted
the burning of the Bishop
of Zaragoza, or so
the story goes. Now it's a hot
tourist spot in season, but
in mid-December the bar
is lined with factory workers
and day laborers as grey
as cement. The place smells
of cement and of urine,
and no one takes off his coat
or sits down to his sherry—
a queen's drink, as thin and dry
as benzine.
          It is Sunday,
late, and each man drinks alone,
seriously. Down the bar
a midget sings to himself,
sings of how from the starving South
he came, a boy, to this terrible
Barcelona, and ate. Not
all the songs are for himself;
he steps back from the bar,
his potbelly pushed out
and wrapped intricately
in a great, somber cummerbund,
and tells the world who is big,
big in the heart, and big down
here, big where it really counts.

Now he comes over to me,
and it is for me he sings.
Does he want money? I try

to buy him off with a drink,
a bored smile, but again
I hear of his power, of how
the Germans, Dutch, English—all
the world's babies—come to him,
and how on the fields of skin
he struts. "Here," he says to me,
"feel this and you'll believe."

In a voice suddenly thin
and adolescent, I tell him
I believe. "Feel this, feel this . . ."
I turn away from him, but
he turns with me, and the room
freezes except for us two.
I can smell the bitterness
of his sweat, and from the cracked
corners of his eyes see the tears
start down their worn courses.
I say, No, No more! He tugs
at my sleeve, hulking now, and
too big for his little feet;
he tugs and will not let go,
and the others along the bar
won't turn or interfere
or leave their drinks. He gets
my hand, first my forefinger
like carrot in his fist,
and then with the other hand,
my wrist, and at last I can't
shake him off or defend
myself.
       He sits in my lap
and sings of Americas,

of those who never returned
and those who never left. The smell
of anise has turned his breath
to a child's breath, but his cheeks,
stiff and peeling, have started
to die. They have turned along
the bar to behold me
on the raised throne of a torn
plastic barstool, blank and drunk
and half asleep. One by one
with the old curses thrown down
they pay up and go out,
and though the place is still
except for the new rumbling
of the morning catching fire
no one hears or no one cares
that I sing to this late-born freak
of the old world swelling my lap,
I sing lullaby, and sing.

JON LAVIERI

Breakfast at the Golden Egg Cafe

I was thinking about nothing
but those shrink-wrapped wedges
of cake and pie tipping forward in tidy rows
along the dessert-case shelves.
"What would you do if yer wife went lezzie?"
The bloodshot moon of the dishwasher's face
suddenly in mine, voice hushed,
as if he were careful
in choosing a confidant. I cursed again
whatever it is in me a stranger like this
finds open. I did my best to evaporate
out of another dead conversation,
but he lights a Lucky Strike
and has me by the ashtray.
"Got it from her uncle she did it with a nigger."

I almost thank him for that much,
for letting me see enough of an ex-wife
finding a sweetness at last in a woman's skin
dark as a midnight he could never begin to navigate.
His jaw was cocked to go on
when a blind man came ticking
through the door behind his cane,
and the dishwasher's jaw stayed down
but his eyes followed the man to his seat.
"Nobody knows when they're goddam lucky," he said.
"Know what I do first thing every morning?"
I looked at the menu for an answer.
"I get up and kiss that cross on the wall!"
His small arm shoots up, out, pointing,
as if I should see the crucifix there,
bearing the dishwasher's favorite little jesus,
his eyes glinting like false gems
searching mine for a sign that I can see
where our salvation lies—
between the cheesecake and pecan pie.

Zarzyski Stomachs the Oxford Special
with Zimmer at the Ox Bar & Grill

Donning his bronc-stomper black hat, cock-eyed
        the morning after reading range rhymes
            in Montana, Zimmer swears out loud
                his belly's tough as whang leather,
            reckons his grease count's a skosh low,
        and it behooves us, here in cattleland,
                to brunch on cow—no quiche,
            no veggie omelet or henfruit Benedict
when Zimmer's craving beeve, a hoof-'n'-horn
                dogie-puncher dose of B-12
                to prod toward procreation
two brain cells the whiskey failed to pickle.

            Zarzyski thinks Zimmer figures
                rare steak and eggs a pair
till he catches Zimmer's eyes, ruminating
behind the stained menu—that devious gleam.
            Zimmer has brains on the mind.

            Zimmer has brains on his mind
and Zarzyski knows too well The Zimmer Dictum:
        what suits one P.Z., damned straight tickles
            another P.Z. plum pink. Sure as shit
                and shootin', like a gunslinger
demanding redeye, crusty-throated Zimmer hollers
            "Bring us hombres brains and eggs."
        And the waitress relays Zimmer's whimsy
            to a fry-cook big enough to eat hay
        and dirty-up the floor. In short-order lingo
            she yells, "these boys *need em*, Sam—
            these Z-boys *need em* real awful bad."

Cafeteria in Boston

I could digest the white slick watery mash,
The two green peppers stuffed with rice and grease
In Harry's Cafeteria, could digest
Angelfood cake too like a sweetened sawdust.
I sought to extend the body's education,
Forced it to swallow down the blunted dazzle
Sucked from the red formica where I leaned.
Took myself farther, digesting as I went,
Course after course: even the bloated man
In cast-off janitor's overalls, who may
Indeed have strayed through only for the toilets;
But as he left I caught his hang-dog stare
At the abandoned platefuls crusted stiff
Like poisoned slugs that froth into their trails.
I stomached him, him of the flabby stomach,
Though it was getting harder to keep down.
But how about the creature scurrying in
From the crowds wet on the November sidewalk,
His face a black skull with a slaty shine,
Who slipped his body with one fluid motion
Into a seat before a dish on which
Scrapings had built a heterogeneous mound,
And set about transferring them to his mouth,
Stacking them faster there than he could swallow,
To get a start on the bus-boys. My mouth too
Was packed, its tastes confused: what bitter juices
I generated in my stomach as
Revulsion met revulsion. Yet at last
I lighted upon meat more to my taste
When, glancing off into the wide fluorescence,
I saw the register, where the owner sat,
And suddenly realized that he, the cooks,
The servers of the line, the bus-boys, all
Kept their eyes studiously turned away
From the black scavenger. Digestively,
That was the course that kept the others down.

216

Elysian Fields

"Champs Elysées of Broadway" says the awning
of the café where, every Sunday morning,
young lawyers in old jeans ripped at the knees
do crosswords. Polyglot Lebanese
own it: they've taken on two more shopfronts
and run their banner down all three at once.
Four years ago, their sign, "Au Petit Beurre"
was so discreet, that, meeting someone there,
I'd tell her the street corner, not the name.
They were in the right place at the right time.
Meanwhile, the poor are trying hard enough.
Outside, on Broadway, people sell their stuff
laid out on blankets, cardboard cartons, towels.
A stout matron with lacquered auburn curls
circles the viridian throw rug
and painted plaster San Martín to hug
a thinner, darker woman, who hugs her
back volubly in Spanish—a neighbor,
I guess, and guess they still have houses.
The man with uncut, browned French paperbacks,
the man with two embroidered gypsy blouses
and three pilled pitiful pairs of plaid slacks
folded beside him on the pavement where
there was a Puerto Rican hardware store
that's been a vacant shopfront for two years
may not. There's a young couple down the block
from our corner: she's tall, gaunt, gangly, Black;
he's short, quick, volatile, unshaven, white.
They set up shop dry mornings around eight.
I've seen him slap her face, jerking her thin
arm like a rag doll's—a dollar kept from him,
she moves too slow, whore, stupid bitch . . . "She's
my wife," he tells a passing man who stops
and watches. If anyone did call the cops

it would be to prevent them and their stacks
of old *Vogues* and outdated science texts
from blocking access to the "upscale bar"
where college boys get bellicose on beer.
"Leave him," would I say? Does she have keys
to an apartment, to a room, a door
to close behind her? What we meant by "poor"
when I was twenty, was a tenement
with clanking pipes and roaches; what we meant
was up six flights of grimed, piss-pungent stairs,
four babies and a baby-faced welfare
worker forbidden to say "birth control."
I was almost her, on the payroll
of New York State Employment Services
—the East 14th Street Branch, whose task it was
to send day workers, mostly Black, to clean
other people's houses. Five-fifteen
and I walked east, walked south, walked up my four
flights. Poor was a neighbor, was next door,
is still a door away. The door is mine.
Outside, the poor work Broadway in the rain.
The cappuccino drinkers watch them pass
under the awning from behind the glass.

MARK SOLOMON

These Are the Streets

These are the streets where I used to walk my rage once it woke
        from the kick I gave the scrap-paper bucket underneath
            The Big Boss Desk I had to sit behind in those days. Leaping
down the back stairs two, three at a time it pulled me, eight stories,
        just to yank me back and forth between the hydrant and the
            lamppost.
            Over there was old Police Headquarters, pistol shops out back
selling handcuffs, ammo, weighted billy clubs. Across the street, first
        Krasilovsky's Safes, next Karl Otto's Tool and Die, and finally Zeke
            the Machinist, wheels within wheels in the window spinning dizzy
combinations driven by thick belts, toothed gears, all off the single, central,
    endless
        worm-screw. And there's the window on Grand and Elizabeth
            where I'd always find
                myself, no jacket in the winter drizzle, staring at the T-shirts—one
of Mussolini, another of Sophia—staring at the long-spouted bright tin
    olive oil cans,
        at the hand-painted cheap espresso cups, staring into the gloomy
            eyes of San
                Gennaro, the blood in its phial gone liquid again, blaspheming
                black
Vesuvius bubbling over behind him. At the bar of The Villa Pensa I
    would lean
        on my elbows, sipping bitter coffee. I would study the twig of
            sugar-crystals
                growing in the golden Fior d'Alpi. I would bite into one of
                    those twisted
black cigars you had to cut in half, smoke circling my eyes and nostrils,
    shrouding
        my anger just enough, Montovani from the hi-fi washing up like
            warm surf
                over soft breasts of white beaches somewhere in my mind.
                Jo-Jo Favale

knew how to take good care of me. The pot of coffee finished, cigar
  chewed through,
      his sweetest waiter, Pepe from Trieste, would show me to the
      corner table —
          flowers, cold glass of water, fresh bread in a basket, cold pats
of butter in a dish of ice, a steaming soup, thick with white beans and
  pastina.
      "Just like Mama make at home," he always said. "Come, take
      your place, Signore.
          I'll go bring some wine." I would smooth the heavy linen
          napkin
open on my lap and bring my chair in close against the table.

Fall in the Equinox Café

Under the thin, chill, rippling light
of the Miller's High Life sign, his hands
show their true colors as, into the peaceful
sleeves of his windbreaker, the blood
withdraws. He can hear it, softly thrumming
the chambers of his heart.

By the dim gazebo in the park
a maple drains the cool green liquor
from her leaves, and leaves them empty,
revealing aboriginal madders,
ardent reds, parched oranges.

He's thinking of dropping his hands at the feet
of the provident nymph in the vermilion mini,
nursing her second double-bourbon
like a warm brown baby.

Report from Nirvana

"Home. Home. I knew it entering. . . ."

RICHARD HUGO

A Place in the Past

Old Man Drunk

He sits before me now, reptilian, cold,
Worn skeletal with sorrow for his child.
He would have lied to her, were he not old:
An old man's fumbling lips are not defiled
By the sweet lies of love. Yet one must be
Skillful to bring it off; that treachery
Whips back to lash the bungler of its art.
He curses his ineptitude of heart.

He knows the quivering eye of youth is blind.
The pale ears, roaring deep as shell, are deaf
To the half-drowning cry of love behind
The skull. His daughter struck him in her grief
Across the face, hearing her lover dead.
He stood behind her chair, he bowed his head,
Knowing that even death cannot prolong
The quick hysteric angers of the young.

I can say nothing. I will see him sit
Under the vacant clock, till I grow old.
The barkeep's wife returns to throw her fit
And pitch us out into the early cold.
I touch his shoulder, but he does not move,
Lost in the blind bewilderment of love,
The meaningless despair that could not keep
His daughter long from falling off to sleep.

Meanwhile, the many faces of old age
Flutter before me in the tavern haze.
He cannot let me see him weep and rage
Into his wrinkled pillow. Face by face,
He grins to entertain, he fills my glass,
Cold to the gestures of my vague *alas*,
Gay as a futile god who cannot die
Till daylight, when the barkeep says goodbye.

225

Fanks

He stopped there after work every day,
it's where he got the bar room smell
he carried around like some people
carry religion. The smoke hung thick
as grief in his clothes and hair,
and the beer announced his lips like a whistle
did a train. I loved it when she'd send me
to fetch him from across the street;
the room would be full of beery dark
and bluster; the doors swung open
easy as sin even for a young girl
like me. I'd find him happy, singing
or reciting some poem he'd got by heart.
He'd teach me a verse or two, give me a swig
from his mug, sparkling and bitter.

RICHARD SPEAKES

Sweet Dreams at the Silver Slipper Tavern

The jukebox was beautiful, thus strange
in those surroundings, as if Matisse designed
a deckhand's one tattoo. I didn't yet know

men and women could be like that tavern,
in their far corners a pulse strong
as the juke's red and blues, with songs

you pay for, and nearer the heart of things,
the slur of torn stools, tables filmed with
the oils of fried fish and hands, a magma

of spilled beer and ash. The air itself
seemed human, rank but familiar, like the one
squabble a couple returns to—the sex,

the money, love's old shoe of rhetoric.
We think he or she is the difference.
We think we need so little, nothing more

than a good time now and then. Now I know
the trouble waiting, like the blonde smiling
at the next table, when we go looking for fun

and find in ourselves what aims to yell,
not sing, to spill beer as well as drink it.
But I was more than confused then—I was ten,

life's innocent bystander walking the road's
white line, or walking the quarter my mother
had me carry to the Wurlitzer when things went

bad or good. Thirty years later I can tell you
each word, every lilt and fall, the trembles in
the two songs she needed time and again. I remember

how it felt to push the red slots like
piano keys indented for your fingers, how they'd
snap and hold a moment before the crisp

release that popped, as if the machine said
yes and slapped its forehead—yes, of course,
it was so obvious one couldn't see it,

Patsy Cline's "Crazy," then "Sweet Dreams."
My parents had a kind of Brownian motion
songs and beer excited, then it was clear

what was stilled by being home cozy with
slippers and dishes drying in the rack.
Grandparents on the wall said *Give up* or

Hang in there, the same thing to my father.
I'd get back from the jukebox with "Crazy"
starting out easy before the grief so good

a boy could almost understand its appeal.
They probably came no closer, but they were
busy with living it, and seemed themselves

startled by things they said or did. Once,
I returned to my father's face dripping beer,
the pitcher empty, and he grinned at it,

talked to it the way he'd talk to engines.
He said, *Look at this bitch, empty as sin.*
Son, go over there and tell the man one more.

And when I came back they were like a storybook
ragged with use, the prince holding in a kiss
the torn princess, almost all the way to "Sweet Dreams."

LYNN EMANUEL

Discovering the Photograph of Lloyd, Earl, and Priscilla

These are the great discoveries of my middle age:
This roadhouse in Omaha where Uncle Lloyd is nursing
Highballs with an ex-G.I. named Earl.
She's here, too, leaving a damp pink parenthesis
On the rim of her glass. The men are bored
But the girl whose name hisses like an iron across damp shirts
Peels open a pack of cigarettes and fills the room with smoke.
I have always wanted a coziness like theirs:
Rain touching the roof and someone trying to explain about Labor—
I might have been the waitress mopping up tips with a damp hand,
The one who loved Earl all those years while toting armloads
Of cobblers made from berries tiny as black caviar.
Tonight in an open window someone's stylus unzips a faint piano.
It must be 1947, Earl slicing salted melon from the rind,
Drinking the juice off his plate and the waitress going home
To count the dresser knobs until she falls asleep.
Tonight I find I envy the rain turning Omaha to daguerreotype,
Mud roads running amber as the veins in bad marble.
It is getting late. In the background beyond Earl and the waitress
There must be gardens. Roses, bowed down by their own heaviness,
Each day grow more perfect and more neighborly.
There must be graves and each separate grave is sending out
Its separate ghost.

LINDA McCARRISTON

The Stardust

18 with our fake ID's we started
hitting the nightspots on Route 1,
dives that are structural to strips

like it anywhere. Half-circle
banquettes—fake velvet, fake leather—
tables the size of the barstools,

the joints packed us in, kids
hungry for the smoky dark mapped out
by a handful of patio candles.

We drank exotic blends—sidecars,
grasshoppers—young women, young
men learning to sit the long hours

on cigarettes, on gin, nothing much
in our stomachs, nothing much to say.
Today on the radio I hear the minor

key *plink* of a xylophone, notes
like a Friday night bar, mixed
with guitar and piano. And a simple

grief comes over me like a drink
for what of ourselves we brought
to those holes, willing to be

adults however it was played:
no boredom too great, no darkness too small,
no drug too strong or too often.

MICHAEL SIMON

The Bar of Forgetfulness

On the island of St. Barthelemy, le Bar de l'Oubli rests,
under its tarp, tourists and locals gathering there:
a *pression* for those who wish to forget,
*cafe au lait f*or those who wish to remember, but

can't, finding some solace in the tarp's shade and movement,
as a cat strides atop it, then settles above the waitress
who looks annoyed, and looks beyond. A car speeds by,
and is incinerated by the sun's dangling fingers. It goes unnoticed.

The sound of boats tapping against their docks breaks
one's heart, as if their aching for release has grown larger
than the dark water which holds them. French floats
in the air like the smell of roasted garlic, or like laughter

from those who can afford it, the way they can afford
to forget, for a week or two, what they left
behind; beyond the waitress who swats at nothing
in front of her face, beyond the tarp and its cat, asleep;

beyond the clouds which have sworn off all movement,
and beyond memory, which lingers, like the waiter
who waits patiently for our laughter's reprieve, before
asking if we wish to remember, or forget.

CHARLES WRIGHT

Bar Giamaica, 1959–60

Grace is the focal point,
                    the tip ends of her loosed hair
Like match fire in the back light,
Her hands in a "Here's the church . . ."
                              She's looking at Ugo Mulas,
Who's looking at us.

Ingrid is writing this all down, and glances up, and stares hard.

This still isn't clear.

I'm looking at Grace, and Goldstein and Borsuk and Dick Venezia
Are looking at me.
                Yola keeps reading her book.

And that leaves the rest of them: Susan and Elena and Carl Glass.
And Thorp and Schimmel and Jim Gates,
                            and Hobart and Schneeman

One afternoon in Milan in the late spring.

Then Ugo finishes, drinks a coffee, and everyone goes away.
Summer arrives, and winter;
                        the snow falls and no one comes back
Ever again,
            all of them gone through the star filter of memory,
With its small gravel and metal tables and passers-by . . .

That's Jazz

JOHN SKOYLES

Kilcullen & Murray's

for Keith Althaus

I take the stool
between the fat lady
bellowing Sophie Tucker
and the Irishman's Al Jolson,
near the obliterating jazz
and the merciful bartender;
because with the clinics,
rest homes, and funeral parlors;
with the news,
and the news behind the news;
with these people who are disappointed
every New Year's Eve,
and who are always facing spring alone,
you get tired of being serious.

BRUCE BERGER

Smoke and Mirrors

Eels elaborately skilled
At vamping the ivories upside down and backwards,
Syncopating the treble, teasing
Tunes from the bass,
Electrifying the silver aquarium
Of a mirror tipped overhead—
Can such dream arms belong

To round after round of song,
To cracked voices fed
By malt and menthols jazzing the back room
Of Marina's Place,
To nights like this, so forgettably pleasing,
To this turquoise-lidded old siren belting out standards,
Keeping the tip jar filled?

Kid Flash

Thanks for the comics.
I hate The Green Lantern.
I hate Kid Flash.
I put them all in the mess hall trash.
When I come home, I will need all new clothes.
These ones are all ripped up.

LOVE, HOWARD
JUNE 29, 1964

Born in the dark, you come back up,
it's a red thing, nightclubbing.
Once, in the Cat's Paw
I fell in love with each man at the bar,
their deeply flanneled arms, their slow bond
with other boys, their back roads,
the women they would never share.

I hate the day coming back
like the horn with its mute inside.
I hate the sheets suspect of tousling
by some other two,
the clothes that seem dampened
by some bygone decade
when you smooth them back on.

Into jazz which makes no children,
into the high wind of the boardwalk,
the aristocracy of a girl's free afternoons,
into the south of boys traveling,
the stucco motel with two-hour coupling shifts,
into the north of men drinking clear
water, to the cafe in New York
where the horn player is always hungry
sweaty, lit in red & you

backing him up, me
in the diamondback dawn, needing
all new clothes, born
in the early morning heat, back up
from camp, I think
I was lonely for everyone in the world.

WILLIAM MATTHEWS

Mingus at The Half Note

Two dozen bars or so into "Better Get It
in Your Soul," the band mossy with sweat,
May 1960 at The Half Note, the rain
on the black streets outside
dusted here and there by the pale pollen
of the streetlights. Blue wreaths
of smoke, the excited calm
of the hip in congregation, the long
night before us like a view and Danny
Richmond so strung out the drums
fizz and seethe. "Ho, hole, hode it,"
Mingus shouts, and the band clatters
to fraught silence. There's a twinge
in the pianist's shoulder but this time
Mingus focuses like a nozzle
his surge of imprecations on a sleek
black man bent chattering across
a table to his lavish date:
"This is your heritage and if you
don' wanna listen, then you got
someplace else you'd better be."
The poor jerk takes a few beats
to realize he'll have to leave
while we all watch before another
note gets played. He glowers dimly
at Mingus, like throwing a rock
at a cliff, then offers his date
a disdained arm, and they leave in single
file (she's first) and don't
look back, nor at each other.
"Don' let me constrain you revellers,"
Mingus says, and then, tamed by his own rage
for now, he kick-starts the band:
"One, two, one two three four."

WILLIAM MATTHEWS

Mingus at The Showplace

I was miserable, of course, for I was seventeen,
and so I swung into action and wrote a poem,

and it was miserable, for that was how I thought
poetry worked: you digested experience and shat

literature. It was 1960 at The Showplace, long since
defunct, on West 4th St., and I sat at the bar,

casting beer money from a thin reel of ones,
the kid in the city, big ears like a puppy.

And I knew Mingus was a genius. I knew two
other things, but as it happened they were wrong.

So I made him look at the poem.
"There's a lot of that going around," he said,

and Sweet Baby Jesus he was right. He glowered
at me but he didn't look as if he thought

bad poems were dangerous, the way some poets do.
If they were baseball executives they'd plot

to destroy sandlots everywhere so that the game
could be saved from children. Of course later

that night he fired his pianist in mid-number
and flurried him from the stand.

"We've suffered a diminuendo in personnel,"
he explained, and the band played on.

PAUL ZIMMER

Romance

This frightened, horny boy
Sits in a jazz club full of
Jungle ferns and leopard skins.

A piano trio is playing,
Dulcet and precise,
"My One and Only Love."

Hank Jones or Billy Taylor?
Al Haig? Ellis Larkins?
It does not matter.

What counts is this song
About something we do not even
Presume to hope for anymore.

Just in time, this wistful,
Tipsy boy hears about love
So sure it lasts a lifetime.

THOMAS LUX

One Meat Ball

You gets no bread with
ONE MEAT BALL
ONE MEAT BALL
ONE MEAT BALL
said the song sung
by the singer
in the famous night club
with the revolving dance floor
atop a famous building
while I ate a steak,
or was it shellfish?
The waiter wore a tux,
the vest of which was stained by gravy.
The song's about a man
who has 15¢ (that's $2.00
in today's money) to eat.
He can afford one meat ball.
He'd like some bread with that.
The waiter in the song
says, with scorn, the above,
or, the singer of the song sings
the waiter saying this.
There's not much else in the song.
There often isn't in songs.
It repeats a lot: redundant
is refrain. The singer
is famous too, I'm told,
and rarely works a room this small,
famous but small. I like the singer,
she's got some pipes, but it's the song
I like the best. Outside,
through the huge banks of tall windows
curving into the ceiling: a million
and twelve stars; and across

and down in every direction: a million
and forty-two lights
of this great city,
in this late, very late, 20th century
in our United States: *You gets no bread with*
ONE MEAT BALL
ONE MEAT BALL
ONE MEAT BALL. . . .

All over the Map

SUSAN MITCHELL

A Story

There is a bar I go to when I'm in Chicago
which is like a bar I used to go to when I lived in New York.
There are the same men racing toy cars
at a back table, the money passing so fast
from hand to hand, I never know who's winning, who's losing,
only in the New York bar the racers sport Hawaiian shirts
while in the Chicago bar they wear Confederate caps
with crossed gold rifles pinned to their bands.
Both bars have oversized TVs and bathrooms
you wouldn't want to be caught dead in,
though some have. Once in the New York bar I watched a film
on psychic surgery, and I swear to you
the surgeon waved a plump hand—
the hand hovered like a dove over the patient's back,
and where wings grow out of an angel's shoulders
a liquid jetted, a clear water, as if pain
were something you could see into like a window.
Later, walking home with a friend
who was also a little drunk, I practiced psychic surgery
on our apartment building, passing my hands
back and forth over the bricks.
I don't know what I expected to happen,
maybe I hoped a pure roach anguish would burst forth.
But there was only the smell that rises out of New York City
in August, a perennial urine—dog, cat, human—
the familiar stench of the body returning to itself as alien.
Sometimes, before stopping in at the Chicago bar,
I would either sleep or go for a walk,
especially in October when the leaves had turned red.
As they swept past me, I thought of my blood
starting to abandon my body,
taking up residence elsewhere like the birds

gathering in feverish groups on the lawns.
In the Chicago bar there were men who never watched TV
or played the video games, mainly from the Plains tribes they
sat in silence over their whiskey, and looking at them,
I could even hear the IRT as it roared through
the long tunnel between Borough Hall and Wall Street,
the screech of darkness on steel.
And it happened one night that a man,
his hair loose to his shoulders, stood up and pulled
a knife from his boot, and another man
who must have been waiting all his life for this
stood up in silence too, and in seconds
one of them was curled around the knife in his chest
as if it were a mystery he would not reveal to anyone.
Sometimes I think my life is what I keep escaping.
Staring at my hands, I almost expect them to turn
into driftwood, bent and polished by the waves,
my only proof I have just returned from a long journey.
The night Tom Littlebird killed Richard Highwater
with a knife no one knew he carried, not even
during the five years he spent at Stateville,
I thought of men and women who sell their blood for
a drink of sleep in a doorway or for a bus ticket
into a night which is also a long drink to nowhere,
and I thought of the blood I was given
when I was nineteen, one transfusion for each year of my life,
and how I promised myself,
if I lived, I would write a poem in honor of blood.
First for my own blood which,
like the letter that begins the alphabet,
is a long cry AAAAH! of relief.
Praise to my own blood which is simple

and accepts almost anything.
And then for the blood that wrestled
all night with my blood
until my veins cramped and the fingers of one hand went rigid.

Praise to the blood that wanted to remain alone,
weeping into its own skin,
so that when it flowed into me, my blood contracted
on the knot in its throat. For you
who raised a rash on my arms
and made my body shiver for days, listen,
whoever you are, this poem is for you.

Angels and the Bars of Manhattan

for Bruce

What I miss most about the city are the angels
and the bars of Manhattan: faithful Cannon's and the Night Cafe;
the Corner Bistro and the infamous White Horse;
McKenna's maniacal hockey fans; the waitresses at Live Bait;
lounges and taverns, taps and pubs;
joints, dives, spots, clubs; all the Blarney
Stones and Roses full of Irish boozers eating brisket
stacked on kaiser rolls with frothing mugs of Ballantine.
How many nights we marked the stations of that cross,
axial or transverse, uptown or down to the East Village
where there's two in every block we'd stop to check,
hoisting McSorleys, shooting tequila and 8-ball
with hipsters and bikers and crazy Ukrainians,
all the black-clad chicks lined up like vodka bottles on Avenue B,
because we liked to drink and talk and argue,
and then at four or five when the whiskey soured
we'd walk the streets for breakfast at some diner,
Daisy's, The Olympia, La Perla del Sur,
deciphering the avenues' hazy lexicon over coffee and eggs,
snow beginning to fall, steam on the windows blurring the film
until the trussed-up sidewalk Christmas trees
resembled something out of Mandelstam,
Russian soldiers bundled in their greatcoats,
honor guard for the republic of salt. Those were the days
of revolutionary zeal. Haughty as dictators, we railed
against the formal elite, certain as Moses or Roger Williams
of our errand into the wilderness. Truly,
there was something almost noble
in the depth of our self-satisfaction, young poets in New York,
how cool. Possessors of absolute knowledge,
we willingly shared it in unmetered verse,
scavenging inspiration from Whitman and history and Hüsker Dü,
from the very bums and benches of Broadway,

247

precisely the way that the homeless
who lived in the Parks Department garage at 79th Street
jacked in to the fixtures to run their appliances
off the city's live current. Volt pirates;
electrical vampires. But what I can't fully fathom
is the nature of the muse that drew us to begin with,
bound us over to those tenements of rage
as surely as the fractured words scrawled across the stoops
and shuttered windows. Whatever compelled us
to suspend the body of our dreams from poetry's slender reed
when any electric guitar would do? Who did we think was listening?
Who, as we cried out, as we shook, rattled and rolled,
would ever hear us among the blue multitudes of Christmas lights
strung as celestial hierarchies from the ceiling? Who
among the analphabetical ranks and orders
of warped records and second-hand books on our shelves,
the quarterlies and *Silver Surfer* comics, velvet Elvises,
candles burned in homage to *Las Siete Potencias Africanas*
as we sat basking in the half-blue glimmer,
tossing the torn foam basketball nigh the invisible hoop,
listening in our pitiless way to two kinds of music,
loud and louder, anarchy and roar, rock and roll
buckling the fundament with pure, delirious noise.
It welled up in us, huge as snowflakes, as manifold,
the way ice devours the reservoir in Central Park.
Like angels or the Silver Surfer we thought we could
kick free of the stars to steer by dead reckoning.
But whose stars were they? And whose angels
if not Rilke's, or Milton's, even Abraham Lincoln's,
"the better angels of our nature" he hoped would emerge,
air-swimmers descending in apple-green light.
We worshipped the anonymous neon apostles of the city,
cuchifrito cherubs, polystyrene seraphim,
thrones and dominions of linoleum and asphalt:
abandoned barges on the Hudson mudflats;

Bowery jukes oozing sepia and plum-colored light;
headless dolls and eviscerated teddy bears
chained to the grills of a thousand garbage trucks; the elms
that bear the wailing skins of plastic bags in their arms all winter,
throttled and grotesque, so that we sometimes wondered
walking Riverside Drive in February or March
why not just put up cement trees with plastic leaves
and get it over with? There was no limit to our capacity for awe
at the city's miraculous icons and instances,
the frenzied cacophony, the democratic whirlwind.
Drunk on thunder, we believed in vision
and the convocation of heavenly presences summoned
to the chorus. Are they with us still? Are they
listening? Spirit of the tiny lights, ghost beneath the words,
numinous and blue, inhaler of bourbon fumes and errant shots,
are you there? I don't know. Somehow I doubt we'll ever know
which song was ours and which the siren
call of the city. More and more, it seems our errand
is to face the music, bring the noise, scour the rocks
to salvage grace notes and fragmented harmonies,
diving for pearls in the beautiful ruins,
walking all night through the pigeon-haunted streets
as fresh snow softly fills the imprint of our steps.
OK, I'm repeating myself, forgive me, I'm sure brevity
is a virtue. It's just this melody keeps begging to be hummed:
McCarthy's, on 14th Street, where the regulars drink
beer on the rocks and the TV shows "Police Woman"
twenty-four hours a day; the quiet, almost tender way
they let the local derelicts in to sleep it off
in the back booths of the Blue & Gold after closing;
and that sign behind the bar at the Marlin, you know
the one, hand-lettered, scribbled with slogans of love and abuse,
shopworn but still bearing its indomitable message
to the thirsty, smoke-fingered, mood-enhanced masses —
"Ice Cold Six Packs To Go." Now that's a poem.

PETER SEARS

Lip's Lounge

They answer the phone there Lips
and lean on it. Where the tongue
goes to curl the L, I don't know,
but the i is long enough to ride
and the s rolling the p enacts
the word rippling the silence
it reverberates into. My stomach
decides, whatever doesn't have
lips wants them. Even a tongue
wants another tongue all its own.
Mine, alone in the mouth, wants
out. Lips says the bartender to
the phone and my tongue comes
out, hangs out of bed. I get
it back in, I use my hand, then
set my legs off across the room.
I like how they lip along,
how they lean in together on
the pool table and a bank shot
kissed just so the slow roll
slits the pocket clean. I'm
ready now to take the calls,
be the man who does the word.
I want the word. I practice,
curl my legs around the table
legs, inhale, lay the words in
air to air. Someday the word
will come without a sound.

X. J. KENNEDY

In a Prominent Bar in Secaucus One Day

To the tune of "The Old Orange Flute"
or the tune of "Sweet Betsy from Pike"

In a prominent bar in Secaucus one day
Rose a lady in skunk with a topheavy sway,
Raised a knobby red finger—all turned from their beer—
While with eyes bright as snowcrust she sang high and clear:

'Now who of you'd think from an eyeload of me
That I once was a lady as proud as could be?
Oh I'd never sit down by a tumbledown drunk
If it wasn't, my dears, for the high cost of junk.

'All the gents used to swear that the white of my calf
Beat the down of the swan by a length and a half.
In the kerchief of linen I caught to my nose
Ah, there never fell snot, but a little gold rose.

'I had seven gold teeth and a toothpick of gold,
My Virginia cheroot was a leaf of it rolled
And I'd light it each time with a thousand in cash—
Why the bums used to fight if I flicked them an ash

'Once the toast of the Biltmore, the belle of the Taft,
I would drink bottle beer at the Drake, never draught,
And dine at the Astor on Salisbury steak
With a clean tablecloth for each bite I did take.

'In a car like the Roxy I'd roll to the track,
A steel-guitar trio, a bar in the back,

And the wheels made no noise, they turned over so fast,
Still it took you ten minutes to see me go past.

'When the horses bowed down to me that I might choose,
I bet on them all, for I hated to lose.
Now I'm saddled each night for my butter and eggs
And the broken threads race down the backs of my legs.

'Let you hold in mind, girls, that your beauty must pass
Like a lovely white clover that rusts with its grass.
Keep your bottoms off barstools and marry you young
Or be left—an old barrel with many a bung.

'For when time takes you out for a spin in his car
You'll be hard-pressed to stop him from going too far
And be left by the roadside, for all your good deeds,
Two toadstools for tits and a face full of weeds.'

All the house raised a cheer, but the man at the bar
Made a phonecall and up pulled a red patrol car
And she blew us a kiss as they copped her away
From that prominent bar in Secaucus, N.J.

DAVE SMITH

At the Greek's Bar

(Williamsburg, Virginia)

Heavy tables, wood gouged with names, some dead on ridges
    in Korea, booths yet bearing their hot tunes
        on wall-boxes for music (night flares
          in cheek-to-cheek dreams),
            a boy like me

        woke alive, the flash of her exploding red
    cardigan hooked his eye, she no more than the thin
  thrush singing down Gloucester Street. On his arm
           then, no moves impossible, beer-scum floor
          dragging like deep snow,
          but nights

          prickle the skin like a rash. Place memory:
    bolt, dance, sweat for the joy lost. Your father found
your mother here. Your name was with the Greeks. *Before.*

    Before what?
        Vietnam.

JUAN FELIPE HERRERA

Iowa Blues Bar Spiritual

Little Tokyo bar—

ladies night, smoky gauze balcony, whispering. Tommy Becker,
makes up words to "La Bamba"—request by Hard Jackson,

mechanic on the left side of Paulie, oldies dancer, glowing
with everything inside of her, shattered remembrances, healed

in lavender nail polish, the jagged fingernail tapping. So
play it hard above this floor, this velvet desert. I want

the Titian ochre yeast of winter, keyboard man, fix your eyes
on my eyes and tell me, handsome, how long will I live?

How many double-fisted desires, crushed letters, will I lift
in this terrain? And this rumbling sleeve, this ironed flint

of inquisitions and imaginary executors, where shall I strike,
what proud stones? Will this fauna open for me, ever, this fuzz

anointed beak inside the bartender's mirrors, etched doves,
a cautious spiral Harley tank, hissing, this Indian bead choker on
    Rita's neck?

How long shall we remain as wavy reflections,
imitators of our own jacket's frown? Who shall awaken first?

Margo Fitzer, the waitress? I will say, Queen Margo, sing to me
stoic princess of slavering hearts, three faint lines creased

on your satin belly, toss our planet onto your umber lacquer tray,
too empty now; make the earth spin its dog rhapsody, erotic

through this silvery off-ramp and flake, unfurl. We tumble across
this raceway in honey-glazed traces, our arms ahead, the hands

flying to Ricky's Ice Cream Parlour, outside. I want to own one
someday, maybe on Thirty-Second Street. You will see me

in my gelled waved hair, my busy wrists—so fast, a clown's
resolute gloves, dipping faster than finger painting—except

I'd be stirring milk and the light chocolate foam of love, churning,
burning this sweet spirit, more uncertain, than the celestial

sheaths above the prairie frost. See the boy coming, they chide,
leaning, how he crosses his legs, his eyes dreaming, sideburns

just shaved clean. He weighs the sour slate on his father's breath;
perfume, fortune, cards left on the bleeding table. Milo Wilkens,
    drummer

at the curve, strokes his nipples with his arms as he hits the high hat.
Somewhere in the back rooms, I know, a shrine, orange sponge
    cushions,

two toilets and a wire wound wicker box, to leave flowers, occasional
offerings by the Johnson County dudes, detasslers in jersey ties.

Talk no more, enjoy. Darling singer, let your starry blouse sway me,
steal this fresh peach half from its amber juice; I want the moon

in this nectar, too. The flashing cymbals, feverish. Who can strike
a votive candle, love, or sleep in this electronic night? Just listen

to the two-part harmony, laughter, peeling beyond the cemetery, beyond
the Iowa river—where the spike hat rooster bristles his tiny ears,

bows his head, and sips from the dark cannister under the carved pearl-stone.
And then, returns. Let us drink, salute the bright spokes of meal, the dying

wands of river blossoms, grandmother's sacred hair; listen, her soprano
owl, her bluish melody, so thin. Another glass please, we shall dance

once again, our eyebrows smearing against each other's cheekbones, loud
with a Midwest sweat, a cantata from the cross-hatch amp, click it.

Click it, for wild kind rain, forgiving seasons, for the blushed bread
of our shoulders and thighs, this night, everyone is here. Even
     Jeff Yoder

came all the way from Illinois, to fill a bucket with passion, ruffled,
thick. O Sax player with a jail needle tattoo, leap onto this wet pavement,

call my lonesome tempest heart, its buried mother's kiss, bless us
in staccato, with quivers of oak branch greenness, and sparrow longings

riff over this brutal sky, give us your bell filled, conjure your tropic,
our lover's breath. Blues bar dancers, jangling gold popcorn, chord makers,

opal-eyed Suzie in a flannel shirt; we beckon the spark, the flaring
this lost body to live.

Ted's Bar and Grill

for Russell Rock

Every night at this place
with one pool table, one pinball machine
we shuffle our greasy boots
up to the bar where Jeannie serves up drinks
with her long blond hair and nice ass.
She's engaged to "a good guy—
he don't hang out in bars"
and she don't have no trouble handling the drunks
because she's so sweet even the drunkest pigs
get shamed by her blushes.

And there's this retarded guy Herbert
with a screwed up face
who can't talk right and drools a lot.
He's always trying to pick up Fat Mary
who needs two bar stools, one for each cheek.
She's always telling him
that she'll bring her boyfriend in
and every time she does
he puts on his sad dog face and starts to moan.
Nobody can stand the noise
so we end up dragging him out the door.
We all know Mary ain't got no boyfriend
and she's lonely as hell
and we're all waiting for the night
she'll get drunk enough so Herbert don't seem retarded
and take him home with her.

Then there's Marty
who just about owns the pool table—
nobody can beat him and no one will play him

but he won't go nowhere else to play.
And old Ted the owner
he just raised prices again and we're pissed
but it's hard to bitch at Jeannie
and Ted hardly comes around anymore
except to kick us out and close up.

Not much excitement here—
not since Jerry kicked the shit out of his boy
when he came in all high on dope
to try and borrow his old man's car.
That was some fight—but a drinker always beats a doper,
everybody knows that.

When the bar closes, I drift on home
and go to bed. Some days I feel
real stupid about myself and my drinking
and can't fall asleep.
I think about going in to work
with a head on again.

I got to stop hanging out at Ted's.
Some nights I try to stay home after work
but then I start thinking
that maybe I'll miss something—
that maybe somebody will beat Marty
or pick up Jeannie or kick Ted's ass
or maybe Herbert will really pick up Mary
walk out the door holding her hand
looking back at me with his goofy face
finally smiling
and twisting my own sour mouth
into a grin.

Bad Manners

Guys with names like 8-Ball
live in this bar. The songs on the box
might sound familiar somewhere else,
but here they're dirty, almost
not sound at all. They blend in
to the other noises, the bottles,
the voices, the toilet that's flushed
only when someone
doesn't want to be heard.

As the night sails away
the patrons float above the floor,
as if to touch the ground
would be bad manners. Touch
of any kind is wrong—
it happens only in fights
and when money changes hands,
changes into something more

comfortable, wait here, I'll be
right back, watch my drink, don't
let it spill on the floor.

DAVID BAKER

8-Ball at the Twilite

for Ed Byrne

The team of Budweiser horses
circling the clock above the bar
must have run a thousand miles already tonight.
What a great place they must want to go,
to work so hard in the smoky air. They've kept on running
though our game fell apart, though the music turned
bad, even though the cowboys at the corner booth
slugged it out over a halter-
topped waitress and had to leave.

It's late now and we should go too.
But we've got one more quarter on the table-edge,
pressing our luck, and half a pitcher
still cool enough to drink.
Connie Francis may say she loves us, if we stay.
So we pass the nub of chalk between us again,
rubbing the last of it over our tips
as a new rack of balls explodes,
running hard for the far green corners.

JAMES HAUG

Pool Is a Godless Sport

I like the articulate crack
the cue ball makes
on impact, how it drops
what it's after and backspins back,
the chalk skids
on its bald surface, blue
and hard as water
or your eye, keen straight
down the line of the poolstick,
how the clogged air of lies
and smoke clears as you circle
the table, the next shot
plump on the rail, a duck.
You're on a roll, playing
collisions of intent and dumb luck.
We don't talk as I gather
a new game in the rack;
no one's put down quarters.
We could shoot hours here.
The bartender yawns and looks on,
pinball bangs a free ball.
We play off the angles, combinations,
the felt before each break
fresh as promise,
and let the rolling geometry
plot our next move.

LAURE-ANNE BOSSELAAR

Letter from Jake's Place, Durango

Dear K,

I know the fat lady won't come
to clear the table, she's leaning
over the bar, arms buried
under tired breasts, talking to a biker.

I push the plates away, grits
and tepid beer. This place
is thick with dust. I'll stay here,
it's a good place, dark enough

to forgive myself: I long for home again.
This time for a rainless summer day
in Antwerp, seagulls swearing at tugboats
pulling ships back from the sea.

Along the quays, the Scheldt river
swells with the North Sea tides:
sweet waters mingle with salt.
An egret slips its neck into

that thickness, gobbles an eel
and rises: a ripple, a crease
in the sky. Not a ripple in the river
though, only summer waves so

languorous you can actually feel them
suck up and come down again,
licking hulls and banks
slick with seaweed and mussels.

I long to watch your hand dip
into cones of newspaper, greasy

with hot fries, and wipe the cool
Duvel beer foam from your mouth.

My lips are heavy with Flemish,
the guttural sounds of the lowlands:
Oh, take me away from this sidewalk café
to a hotel, any hotel — hurry! —

but with a view of the Scheldt.

Kate and Gary's Bar, Red River, New Mexico

Just over the mountains from Eagle Nest
where the glacial maw ground out a valley
and oceans of gold aspens surge around steep
boulder fields and islands of evergreens and
the collapsing ghost town where hippies hole up
you come to Red River: a string of bars
and curio shops, all pine planks and logs.
The river rattles rocks behind the town.
Farther on, towards Questa where the Rockies open
to volcanic plains, a huge gray slag heap
slides towards the river from the molybdenum mine.
The town makes no claim on eternity,
a mere moment in the granite gorge
shadowed by whistling crags and forests
beside a river carving out canyons
eating its way to the sea.

Kate's son drove me into town,
picked me up off the road from Questa,
so I had her roast beef special and a beer.
She pulled a chair from the edge of the dance floor,
watched my Adam's apple bob with beer and studied
my backpack and sleeping bag leaning by the door.
"What do you do, anyway?" she asked. "You're no drifter."
"I write poetry," I said. She smiled,
and pushed her bifocals back up her nose.
"I knew you did something like that.
Grace," she called behind the bar
to the long-legged girl setting up drinks,
"bring our friend another Coors."

RICHARD HUGO

The Only Bar in Dixon

Home. Home. I knew it entering.
Green cheap plaster and the stores
across the street toward the river
failed. One Indian depressed
on Thunderbird. Another buying
Thunderbird to go. This air
is fat with gangsters I imagine
on the run. If they ran here
they would be running from
imaginary cars. No one cares
about the wanted posters
in the brand new concrete block P.O.

This is home because some people
go to Perma and come back
from Perma saying Perma
is no fun. To revive, you take 382
to Hot Springs, your life savings
ready for a choice of bars, your hotel
glamorous with neon up the hill.
Is home because the Jocko
dies into the Flathead. Home because
the Flathead goes home north northwest.

I want home full of grim permission.
You can go as out of business here
as rivers or the railroad station.
I new it entering.
                    Five bourbons
and I'm in some other home.

RICHARD HUGO

Death of the Kapowsin Tavern

I can't ridge it back again from char.
Not one board left. Only ash a cat explores
and shattered glass smoked black and strung
about from the explosion I believe
in the reports. The white school up for sale
for years, most homes abandoned to the rocks
of passing boys—the fire, helped by wind
that blew the neon out six year before,
simply ended lots of ending.

A damn shame. Now, when the night chill
of the lake gets in a troller's bones
where can the troller go for bad wine
washed down frantically with beer?
And when wise men are in style again
will one recount the two-mile glide of cranes
from dead pines or the nameless yellow
flowers thriving in the useless logs,
or dots of light all night about the far end
of the lake, the dawn arrival of the idiot
with catfish—most of all, above the lake
the temple and our sanctuary there?

Nothing dies as slowly as a scene.
The dusty jukebox cracking through
the cackle of a beered-up crone—
wagered wine—sudden need to dance—
these remain in the black debris.
Although I know in time the lake will send
wind black enough to blow it all away.

Real Characters

A Story Often Told in Bars:
The *Reader's Digest* Version

First I was born and it was tough on Mom.
Dad felt left out. There's much I can't recall.
I seethed my way to speech and said a lot
of things: some were deemed cute. I was so small
my likely chance was growth, and so I grew.
Long days in school I filled, like a spring creek,
with boredom. Sex I discovered soon
enough, I now think. Sweet misery!

There's not enough room in a poem so curt
to get me out of adolescence, yet
I'm nearing fifty with a limp, and dread
the way the dead get stacked up like a cord
of wood. Not much of a story, is it?
The life that matter's not the one I've led.

PETER SEARS

Harvey Wallbanger

With a good old lousy Rita Hayworth Chinese
smuggling movie on, why do I watch tanker
spill news below tailfeathers of a stuffed

Schlitz peacock in my dump bar? Because I
like taking soundings of the bottomless
muck of the world. Because I like to pour

Another shot of crap to dump on my head
for the jerk I have backed myself into. Oh
I wish people were here so I could wish

They would leave. Tell me how wretched we are,
and I will match you, low for low, jerk for
jerk, and to our snow piled street declare:

Peace to Harvey Wallbanger and everyone I've
lived by blindly crabbing and peace to people
I'll never meet being from around here only.

JOHN REINHARD

For the Barmaid
Unhappy with the Size of Her Breasts

She brings you a beer and sad eyes
that she says are bigger than . . . she looks
down. This is a slow night in bars
across America. Every husband has gone
home to his wife. So she sits with you.
Calls you sensitive. Complains that
her nipples feel too close to the rest
of her body, that she wants some space.
This part of her out front of everything else.

You figure a story here won't hurt, and tell her
you're just lately a farmer who's sown
his first field of oats, driven his first
antique John Deere tractor. Tell her
these oats are already rising, and all
the old Norwegians, snoose trickling
from their mouths, look
at the field and you and then
say, "Take pictures," as though no one
will believe this, how your rows waver
and stray from expected lines.
Even the birds stay away.

At this point, the barmaid buttons
the top of her blouse. Seems close
to tears. You keep going.

Tell her that you like your rows for all
their unevenness. And when aerial
photographs are taken, your field
will become famous in agricultural offices
all over the midwest. Before long,
the old farmers will be back, their chins

clean, to see exactly how it was
you planted. The moral of this,
you tell the barmaid, is that
what is ours is good. That you
have sown your oats and they
are lovely, wherever they lie.
That her breasts are lovely as well
and that size only matters in silhouettes.
At this she smiles. It is the sort of smile
you have skidded over icy roads to reach. It is
as though her entire body curves upward.

Mitch

Mitch in his down and out glory;
the bartender's ear tilts it in
night after night,
how Mitch risked his neck
for a stacked deck
and worn-down luck became his lady.

As he pours the wounding booze,
the bartender traces the bar
for his evening's dream:
Mitch in a six-gun stagger,
Cherokee wine to flood out the pain,
death sweeping up tubercular blood
but Mitch's smile, ten gallon, frayed
too big for the bin.

ALVIN GREENBERG

Old Sonny

took old sonny into a bar one time
and he was good, i mean he just laid
down on the floor beside my stool and stayed
there, while this guy on the stool next to mine
stared and stared, then wanted to know what kind
of dog that was. a yellow lab, i said,
and he said, no, it ain't, and i was afraid
for a minute there that suddenly i'd find
myself entangled in some stupid barroom brawl
for the first time in my life, battered, bloody,
down on my knees on the floor—and all for a dog.
life, friends, is difficult. and that's not all:
you're always coming up against some moody
son-of-a-bitch looking for someone to slug,

but i didn't give an inch: he's a yellow lab,
i said (because he is), and this old guy
drained his beer and looked me in the eye
and said, again, he ain't. friends, i'm misled
by so many things that i've just got to grab
at the rare, pure, simple truth that comes my way.
now i don't like to see blood shed, especially my
own, but dammit, a yellow lab's a yellow lab,
even if mixed, a little, with golden retriever,
and so after a little pause i said, yes, he is,
and drank my beer and waited to eat my teeth.
but he just paid and left. friends, did you ever
know truth to have such a moral bark as this?
speak, always speak up: a dog's an act of belief.

The Poet Flexes His Magnanimity

Shot pool with a philosopher last night
for the price of beers. He had a lovely girl
and most of a Ph.D., but no sense
of humor. I beat him three times before
he cursed, glanced back at bored Lovely
and complained, *Why can't I win?*
I'm older and smarter than you.
How old? I asked him. Nearly thirty.
How smart? He didn't laugh, but Lovely did
and I won again. He knew enough
to feel uneasy for letting her sit
through his losses. But Lovely dismissed it.
I know, she shrugged. *You have to beat him.*
Then he did once, and he got a wind in him.
Don't you write (lip-curling pause, glance back)
poetry? and, before I could answer,
said, *Yeah, never understood*
the stuff. I twitched my lip at him
for that, for poetry. But I knew
what he meant. I never understood
the stuff myself. And still I know
(and not to brag, but to observe,
to *philosophize* even) had I not
been drinking on his nickel, had I not
some poet's love for that unlovely,
embittered, most human of bastards,
for the price of a sheet of white
and a dash of ink I could have sonneted
Lovely away as slick as a clean straight shot
on an open pocket.

Bar Story

How'd I know this kid was anybody's wife?
All I know's the eye she give me. It was rover,
one of these. So I says, "What's your pleasure?"
But this big guy, must be forty, come up
out of the john all in a huff. Steps up.
Here's where things took a turn. She just goes, "Oops,"
and puts her fingers to her lips, you know,
where I can see the ring, but with her eye
on him, like, Yall think yall can handle this?

You been in bars like what this was. It was
big ferns in crocks, fat salesmen in old plaids—
the local girls got party dresses on.
I had me my stitched cowboy shirt. I'm there
trying this credit card . . . which was a gift,
but that's another story. Main thing is,
it's not the kind of place you look for trouble.

So: she come back at me like he's still gone,
"Frank here and me, we're on our honeymoon.
We're celebrating. What's your name?"

                                    "I'm tired."
Frank says, half sideways, looking more at me.

Something about Frank tickled me. I said,
"Frank, please. Let me buy yall some champagne."
And I just grinned, because it's something here
I had to watch. "Post. Daryl Post's the name."
That was the name I went by, on the card.

"Daryl!" she says. "And I'm Cheryl. That's weird.
Don't you think so? Him Daryl and me Cheryl?"

"Mr. Post, you will excuse us," Frank says,
like he owned the steps to heaven can't nobody

climb but college boys. Thing is: Cheryl's bound
to been a barroom tart since she was twelve.

I know this girl. I know: she married wrong,
she knows it, she knows I know, and old Frank
must just be finding out. That's where we are
now while I'm buying us champagne. I made
the toast: "To wedlock, and the padlock. Here's
to locks." So Cheryl giggles and drinks up.

But Frank just looks off, sadlike, and don't drink.
I thought that toast might tickle Frank, a man
with education. I said, "Frank. Here's locks.
Here's keys that go round easy in the tumblers."

This time Frank looked down into his glass,
and Cheryl didn't laugh. It's like the two of 'em
caught wind of a bad fart. So I said, "Frank,
have I got spinach in my teeth? Am I . . ."

All of a sudden Frank says to the bartender
to call the police! Which he does! Look at this:
I dressed up nice and come there like I did
because I figured it won't be no police,
and now Frank's took it on himself to call.
And give my name. When I ain't done one thing
but bought champagne and made some conversation.

Well: I took this here. I used to go out
with an ER nurse and meeting her at work
one time I picked this up. It's whatchacall . . .
a surgical knife. I carry it. Now, what
I done with Frank, I took this out, I yanked
his shirtwaist to his chin, and I just
opened him, up the front. That's all I did.
I just opened him up the front, that's all.

Pragmatists

The Friday night women bare their throats
and half their breasts; the men throw back
their heads to emphasize mirth—except for one
who stumbles from the bar alone, the jut
of his belly almost childlike, and cozies up
to the pay phone like the woman
he'd persuade to meet him later on.
He tries a repertoire of enticements,
jokes as she refuses each one.

You, though, have commandeered
the house phone—does the woman at the desk
also admire you, cradling the receiver
between shoulder's hunch and cheek,
hop angled to the door-frame? From here,
I see only a slice of you—stab
of a workman's hand, tassel of lashes—
too much to be practical, as you'd like.

Near me, a woman stands transfixed
by the chandelier hanging its icy bulk
inches from our heads. Its thick curves
and tongues of glass seem too heavy
to transport anyone, but she gazes, rapt,
then explains her mother has a chandelier
like this she loves to take apart
and clean. Take apart? Each section unhooks
easily, then returns, transparent.
Her date leads her out on a linked arm.
Outside, the vapor lights deny the night;
the cloud cover's shot with the last signs
of storm. I point out the chandelier cleaner,

but her story doesn't amuse you, stalled
by the tail of hair riding her shoulder,
the curve of her head to the man's ear.
I touch your sleeve—a pragmatist,
knowing no one in this town but you.

LYNN EMANUEL

The Night Man at the Blue Lite

Luther Benton is talking to his heart again.
She can see it through the smeared window
of the Blue Lite Motel & Lounge, his mouth
ajar at bored Rita, the waitress, lifting
a cigarette to the scarlet crescent of her smile.
He is talking to his heart while the grillman
loses himself in the news and in one corner
of Ely the juke delivers the goods. I love him
in love—my grandfather's hired man. Bringing
in the morning coffee, he would say with a whistle
Be still my heart and then succumb to one
or another bad line of credit that came in
to work on a drunk under the liquid stare
of a ten-point buck. Night after night
he'd peer at the darkened windows, the smear
of moon, listening to the lovers groaning
over the oiled switches of his remembrance
until above the Snake Range a dawn
of unrequited love rose like the Kingdom of Heaven.
No one for miles. No one
in those golden streets, but Luther.

Fun

"All I want is to have a little fun
Before I die," says the man next to me
Out of nowhere, apropos of nothing. He says
His name's William but I'm sure he's Bill
Or Billy, Mac or Buddy; he's plain ugly to me,
And I wonder if he's ever had fun in his life.

We are drinking beer at noon on Tuesday,
In a bar that faces a giant car wash.
The good people of the world are washing their cars
On their lunch hours, hosing and scrubbing
As best they can in skirts and suits.
They drive their shiny Datsuns and Buicks
Back to the phone company, the record store,
The genetic engineering lab, but not a single one
Appears to be having fun like Billy and me.

I like a good beer buzz early in the day,
And Billy likes to peel the labels
From his bottles of Bud and shred them on the bar.
Then he lights every match in an oversized pack,
Letting each one burn down to his thick fingers
Before blowing and cursing them out.

A happy couple enters the bar, dangerously close
To one another, like this is a motel,
But they clean up their act when we give them
A Look. One quick beer and they're out,
Down the road and in the next state
For all I care, smiling like idiots.
We cover sports and politics and once,
When Billy burns his thumb and lets out a yelp,
The bartender looks up from his want-ads.

Otherwise the bar is ours, and the day and the night
And the car wash too, the matches and the Buds
And the clean and dirty cars, the sun and the moon
And every motel on this highway. It's ours, you hear?
And we've got plans, so relax and let us in—
All we want is to have a little fun.

KURT BROWN

Wide World of Sports

He leans back to stuff
some bills into his pocket and falls
off his stool like a drunk
falling off his stool—
heavy, clumsy, pathetic.
Struggling into his seat again
he lights a cigarette:
Holy Jesus Christ, he says, Holy Jesus Christ
then glances over his shoulder
to glare at the woman whose fat laugh
rolls through the room.
He's not a bomb ready to go off.
He's not even a dangerous character.
Above him on TV
men in baseball jerseys
prance upon a perfect carpet of clipped grass—
someone spits in Cincinnati,
someone lean and muscular and young.
Fucking bum, he mumbles
at the rippling jaw, the powerful shoulders
that launch a homer
into the city over the left-field wall,
a city that lifts its hands
in adulation. Fucking
bum, he says again and turns to face
the man on his left
who ignores his baleful stare.
That's it That's all she wrote We're outta here
the man on the stool announces
to no one in particular
then spots a friend just coming in the door
wearing a canvas boating cap
and dilapidated sneakers.
Hey Sully, he shouts, Hey Sully

Here's looking up your old address!
as the TV sorts its images,
plays a beer commercial
resolving over his head into a wishful dream:
men in a bar laughing, drinking,
beautiful women perched on stools beside them.

SUSAN WOOD

Knowing the End

for Lee Abbott

It's like knowing a girl named Roxy,
you said, to hear the plot before you see
the movie. Say a man is sitting in a bar in Cleveland
late some night and he's lost count
how many shots of Black Jack
he's knocked back and he's too many sheets
to the wind to care. The Indians, picked
to win the East, are locked up
in the cellar once again. They've thrown away
the key. The bartender asks him if he wants
another and he says, Sure, why not, after all
he's Chief of the Bureau of Lost Causes.
Then down the bar he sees her, eyes
green as the underside of a new leaf, a mini-skirt
hiked up to show six inches of white thigh
creamy as a wedding cake. He likes the way
her red hair swings against her back
when she bends to light a Kool, then cocks it
in the air and sips some fancy drink, maybe
a sloe gin fizz. He sidles over and offers
to buy her a refill. She's seen a few like him
too many, but she'd like to have some fun.
He's already a goner. She's a secretary
who wanted to be an actress, but what the hell,
L.A.'s too far away and, besides, she's heard
those stories of the casting couch. She's saving
for Club Med. Her name's Roxy, she says, and right away
he sees the future: maybe a few nights
in an apartment with two cats and lady's lingerie
sprouting like Queen Anne's lace on the bathroom's
snowy field and before long she's working overtime
and coming home at 2 A.M. Someone calls

and when he answers, they hang up. Pretty soon
he's sitting on this stool again and he's lost
count how many shots of Black Jack he's knocked back.
He knew it all the time, he tells the bartender.
Isn't he the Chief? Hey, he wrote the script.
Let's face it, friend, it wouldn't take a girl
like that to break his heart. Anything could
do it. Still, wasn't it sweet those nights they lay
entangled on her flowered sheets and wasn't he brave
to believe it? It's the hope we have
to live with, why we keep on waking up
to think today neither the Indians nor love
will disappoint, though now we know every plot
by heart and still, before we're ready
the climax comes, the screen goes dark.

On the Strip

Coldburn Vertigo

There was a wind of faces
passing in the street,
a chill rippling of bodies in the glass,
eyes that closed or burned
when he looked into them.
The women were angry or stoned,
so were the men.
There were no children.
The old ones leaned into the wind
or hung their heads over the pavement
as though looking for a single blade
of grass or tuft of weed
that might return them to the home
their bodies had been.

A woman dropped her purse
in a crosswalk. He bent
to pick it up. She screamed
in his face. His heart shrank,
his body went gray and small,
his eyes, round and bald
in the wind. He darted
among the trod and footfall
gurgling and cooing over cracks
and stained slabs.

Then he found a door
under spitting blue neon,
the Lion's Den, the Lamb's Pen,
he wasn't sure. He opened the door,
took twelve or fourteen steps,
and settled himself on a stool
in the smokey blue gloom.
In the mirror across the bar,

a small man in a helmet of feathers
closed his burning eyes.

Vertigo reeked from some ashtray
in his brain. He drifted up
and rippled like a ribbon of smoke
on that warm air that was breath
turned to words turned to surf,
the hiss and roar, the undertone
in all the rooms wearing at the thin,
sheer membrane of the eardrum,
the swirl and rush in the blood
that is the wind in the streets,
waves working at every shore.

Who was he but this man adrift,
this man turned into a pigeon
drawn by desire and contagion
to streets and gutters and smokey rooms,
the fascinating city, away from the boy
whose mother loved him, the boy
who held the heads of the electric cat,
the tender dog against his chest
because they consented, because they seemed
to understand the simple rhythm
of his heart, the choice he had made
with his hands.

When he opened his eyes,
things went from bad to worse
to a kind of cold burning
in which he found himself
hovering in the dark
near the ceiling just above

the blue shower pouring from the spotlight
onto the naked, dancing woman.
She was not really a woman
but a holograph of a woman
jerking to a drumbeat that erased her
and left this cold, still-lovely body
burning in her place.

She was less than a woman,
he was less than a man.
In something less than this life,
drifting down through the music
in his garment of feathers,
he alighted among the glitter
in her hair, and his eyes
were two more points of blue light
burning, blue gas flames
in some far room.

And just when he thought it was over,
just when the cymbals shimmered
like water on fire
and the small room of his mind dimmed,
he felt her hand around him,
his bird-heart beating with the drum
in the room gone red,
and she held him to her breast
and danced as though she were real,
as though even this moment mattered.

Draft of the Smoky Life

As the store windows light up
in the downhearted district
where children are never seen,
men collect at The Town Pump,
our faces orange in the sunset,
each of us holding out
the meat of his hand to be stamped
as though to register
our stand against oblivion.

Tracking our reflection
in long mirrors, keeping our appointment
to be cured in smoke.

We sit on fingers
nicked by tools
watching the thighs
of dancers. Our
legs wrap around
chair legs, roads
come down the mountain.
Into the curves each man
tailgates his desire.
But each man tailgates the same
desire. When we enter here

something falls through us
from out of a blue hope.

The air blurred and hoarse,
we get freaky with our own smell,
our flannel shirts stink to hell
of hung fire and beer.

There is no band. We go
into the men's room holding hands.

RICHARD HUGO

Dancer at Kozani's

Through the white chiffon that covered her
we whipped her with our eyes until
she crawled the floor in heat.
When she got up, disrobed and shook
the wall got wet. The lute
that led her shimmy stung her thighs.

Swish of red hair on the floor, twitch
of buttock, breast line clean in shake—
she danced us into war and back
and when the fiddle tied her to a rock
she wiggled free. Her legs were wild
as pillars to a Persian lost in wind.
When far strings tore her from our sight
what vain trout circled in our wine?

We swam out into the smothering night
praying for rain to wash the smoke away.

RUTH ANDERSON BARNETT

Mike's Bar, off I-5, North of Victorville

Among the semis, choppers, the dusty
hulks of the regulars, Dixie
eases the red Pontiac into a slot,
checks the half-light overhead, patting powder
on laugh lines turned to crevices.
Near the entrance, a clutch of truckers
leans on a hood, snickering,
and for a minute, she thinks of leaving—
there's scotch on the kitchen counter, and a radio.
But what man ever kept Dixie from her pleasure?
She crosses the asphalt,
her back as straight as she can make it,

blinks in the doorway, adjusting
to the heavy air, gray and streaked with smoke.
A curtain of beer and sweat,
and from across the room
the crack and rumble of the pocket ball,
then the floor drums with the jukebox,
bass throbbing through her soles, up
into her spine. Hips remembering
the roll and twist, Dixie waits
to make her entrance. Over the bar,
the neon Bud sign flashes like a detour.
She wants the blond young biker bending
above the green of the billiard table, she wants
to be in the backstage dressing room,
tangled in Charley's body, she vamps a little
toward the bar and a few heads turn,
the biker makes his shot, the heads turn back.

As she crosses her knees atop a stool,
her mini-skirt does a shrinking little slither,
cracked leatherette catching her thigh.
She uncrosses her legs, tugs the skirt—
whatever else she's lost, Dixie thinks,
at least she can keep her dignity.

RUTH ANDERSON BARNETT

Dixie Remembers the Runway

All you're doing, to be honest,
is getting out of your dress.
First, you get into it.
Your creation: electric blue, violet,
colors with just a hint of heat.
You didn't stitch it, so no snaps or zippers,
just silk like the sarong
you made yourself in Mother's sewing room.
When the curtain parts, you're seamless,
smooth, an antique marble statue.
You're a class act.
The trick's to pause a moment longer
while their whistles rise like wind.
Then move. They like that,
their breath bringing you to life.
It might amuse you to imagine
your skin humming beneath the hands
of one of them, the blond kid in front—
is this his first time?
He's imagining your mouth around
his name. But you don't want that.
What you want is silk along your thighs.
You pivot to erase their faces
and your flesh begins to purr.
Now the knot at your neck:
you tug gently, and down your back
the cloth shivers, humid air
comes flying in like waves.
Boa feathering your breasts,
you make a last slow sweep,
you don't rush this, you dally
in the silk still clinging at your waist.
At the end of your stroll, your body waits

like a twin you've lost touch with.
The men are bystanders, you hardly need them
when you drop the boa, when you give them
what you came for, letting go the last knots
only you know how to tie.

HEATHER McHUGH

Gig at Big Al's

There's a special privacy on stage.
Wearing little, then less, then
nudity's two silver
high-heeled shoes, I have

to dance, and I dance to
myself: the men are posed at tables just below,
importantly equipped with gazes of assessors
and the paycheck's sure
prerogatives—but they are dreams

I've realized, they are the made-up eyes. No one
knows anyone. I pull down dark around the room.
I turn on sex's juke two-step. I set
foot on the spotlight's

isolated space and grease
a hip and lick a leg. With a whip-
lash of gin in the first row, with
a beer can of bucks in the last, anybody can buy
my solitude (this multiple
circumlocution of crotch). But nobody

can touch me; by the law of California,
I can't "touch myself." So though it's all
complicit, none of it is public—not until

    in one side door
        on his soft shoes
            my lover comes to watch.

MARK WUNDERLICH

Take Good Care of Yourself

On the runway at the Rosy, the drag queen
fans herself gently, but with purpose.
She is an Asian princess, an elaborate wig
jangling like bells on a Shinto temple,
shoulders broad as my father's. With a flick

of her fan she covers her face, a whole
world of authority in that one gesture,
a screen sliding back, all black lacquer
and soprano laugh. The music of this place
echoes with the whip-crack of 2,000

men's libidos, and the one bitter pill
of X-tasy dissolving on my tongue is the perfect
slender measure of the holy ghost,
the vibe crawling my spine exactly,
I assure myself, what I've always wanted.

It is 1992. There is no you yet for me
to address, just simple imperative. *Give
me more. Give.* It is a vision, I'm sure
of this, of what heaven could provide—a sea
of men all muscle, white briefs and pearls,

of kilts cut too short for Catholic girls
or a Highland fling. Don't bother with chat
just yet. I've stripped and checked my jeans
at the door. I need a drink, a light, someplace
a little cooler, just for a minute, to chill.

☾

There is no place like the unbearable ribbon
of highway that cuts the Midwest into two unequal
halves, a pale sun glowing like the fire

of one last cigarette. It is the prairie
I'm scared of, barreling off in all directions

flat as its inhabitants' As and Os. I left
Wisconsin's well-tempered rooms
and snow-fields white and vacant as a bed
I'd wished I'd never slept in. Winters
I'd stare out the bus window through frost

at an icy template of what the world offered up—
the moon's tin cup of romance and a beauty,
that if held too long to the body,
would melt. If I'd felt anything for you then
it was mere, the flicker of possibility

a quickening of the pulse when I'd imagine
a future, not here but elsewhere, the sky
not yawning out, but hemmed in. In her dress
the drag is all glitter and perfect grace,
pure artifice, beating her fan, injuring

the smoky air, and in the club, I'm still
imagining. The stacks of speakers burn
and throb, whole cities of sound bear down
on us. I'm dancing with men all around me,
moving every muscle I can, the woman's voice

mixed and extended to a gorgeous black note
in a song that only now can I remember—
one familiar flat stretch, one wide-open vista
and a rhythm married to the words standing
for what it was we still had to lose.

ANDREA HOLLANDER BUDY

Poem for My Brother, Manager of a Go-Go Bar in Roselle Park, New Jersey

Some night between midnight and three
when the last of the great pinchers
has finished his final drink
and you have taken his keys
and walked him out to the slick
New Jersey street, wet with the glaze
of approaching morning, and told him
to sleep it off in his own back seat,
then walked slowly back to the bar,
picking up debris and trash, tidying
the sidewalk, thinking about tomorrow,
about the girls who don't mean anything
or the greasy spot on the pavement
that is always there, no matter what
the weather, the streetlight out front
the only moon you ever see —
before you step inside and tend
the last of the sweeping and breathe
the last of the evening's smoke,
the music turned down but still on
so you won't be lonely, it would be sweet
if you would remember me, your only sister
ten years older and distant in miles
and habit, living for fifteen years
in the backwoods of a southern state
you've never seen, in a dry county
(where there still are such things)
rubbing the backs of her achy legs
with alcohol to suffocate
the chiggers, as she sits at the edge
of her homemade deck facing east
and thinks of you, as someone might

leaf through a history book and glance
at the pictures of places she had been,
or bends over a child's telescope
taking turns with her son and husband,
and names planets at a glimpse.
Tonight the music here is calm as crickets
and in a minute it is all I'll hear
as I put my son to bed and step out
again to watch the dark grow black
as the moon recedes, while somewhere east
the moon's already tipped her hat and you
have latched the latch and put the keys
in your pocket, whistling, clicking
down the street to your car, glancing back,
thinking that this is the only life
you'd ever wished for or dreamed.

The Road Out

There's an infinity of choices,

But Carlos & Schweidel & I don't know it when we hit on heading
For this bar off Speedway. The road here four lanes

Of sodium vapor lamps & palmettos & shifting accelerations,
Then a parking lot beneath The Blue Note's blinking red neon.
We walk into canned rock 'n' roll where, twenty-five hours a day,

Just as the sign says, three gorgeous coeds
Strip & purr in sexual abandon, or dance bored silly & degraded,
Depending on who you ask. If you bother,

Which we don't. So, as we take out our money,

The bilious little clear-eyed patriot on each dollar
Agrees it is better sometimes to rest
Inside sweet incomprehension, not knowing who you are

When you are a man in the crowd who barks barking his laugh,
When you are an illusion who asks each table to tip her dance.

Better that a biker with tangled beard & leather top hat
Get up when the blue spot invades his heart & lick
A tattered five-dollar bill
So as to paste it more easily

On the sumptuous belly of the woman twitching low now on stage.
It is better, because no one here prays to become someone else,
And if they did, it would only be to beg
Let me, Let me become, Let me become the name of the road out.

Some Enchanted Evening

MARK COX

The Angelfish

Every day at five, the beautiful angelfish stops
at this corner of the tank. He is patient
and knows the bartender will come
with his salt shaker of food.

Every so often he glances around to see
if a certain female angelfish has come in.

He thinks about how if I stare at a woman long enough,
she will either blush or not and I will either blush
or not. It strikes him that fish don't have much weather
to talk about and he wonders if I know my mouth
is opening and closing all the time.

Does he love her? Does she prefer another angelfish
in another section of the huge tank? Will he ever
be happier than this? The bartender sees him now
and smiles and puts his big face up to the glass.

Something dry, the angelfish says, *something very dry*.

SOPHIE CABOT BLACK

Report from Nirvana

(Nightclub Nirvana atop the Great White Way,
1 Times Square Plaza)

Too much piped in air. The elevator receives,
Speeds up the one tunnel it knows
Through garbling floors that light up and sound
As we pass dark offices and nightmaids—

Too long in this place. Even as we sleep
Work is given out. And those of us who cannot sleep
Endure strangers once again, someone
To say words the exact way you waited

All your life to have them said.
We have been here too long. A woman wants
To buy you a drink, another asks for a match.
Pretend you already know this architecture

Was planned with leaving in mind,
To stand on top of, perhaps in love and baying
At the sky, this place we nightly maneuver
Toward the same seat with someone

To spread desire out for. You forget
What you ever knew, high, getting
Higher until everywhere and anything
Can happen. And it's enough.

The Only Dance There Is

Oh no! He's going to *show* it to me—
This gelatinous spore burst like a shot bird's foot—
Splayed, in the nest of his own little egg cup ear. God!
Is it he, or is it I, in my white spikes and levis,
Peeling sweaty red labels off Buds, who becomes
Slowly exposed, a pornographic snap developing
At a While-U-Wate Shak? Is it my turquoise lighter holder,
Or my voice, full of coins and strangulations,
That compels the alcoholics, the men I literally live for,
To repeatedly ask what I want? *Hey! What do you want?*
I know girls who dance in bars and marry, like, firemen.
This man here is so unemployed I could talk to him
All night. I'm saddled on a teetering labrador of lust, drunk
And ready to fill up a station wagon. It is

the *dégringolade* of the species of woman I am—
The curl of my big leg and the smell of that sweat,
Redolent and in that Terrible Vicinity. Here, *let me buy that,*
I am transmigrating in the *def leppard* of my "desire"
And it has happened before, is happening, will happen again,
All of it. It's the old lovemaking in the cemetery routine,
        Johnny.
The last beauty I fell for drank me AND fucked me
Under the table. He said, "Hey there you little redheaded
        sweetiepie, you.
Perfection, my life is an open casket funeral; darling,
Our love is the visitation hour." You heard what he did next.
Frankly I still admire him.
I have nevernever touched myself so well,
Nor could I observe a man jerk off in a sock with such joy.
At times I swear the sex of the earth is the sponge and bedwash for Jesus.
At times I swear I could live with a man I'll call "Tom"

forever: when we met he bound me with Venetian blind cord
And went down on me for roughly nine hours. He delivered
His own daughters' sons. You know how it must be for me.
Drunk in bars, I feel the righteous *ness* of humidity and cherry,
Initials carved in tequila-drenched grains with "surgical
      precision."
We are listing toward the primordial wind and I talk about men
To men. (Once, my hair caught fire in a tavern.
      The man who set it horsewhipped my head, singeing
      His shavebrush Stetson.)
An absolute glance. Tufts of a botched permanent wave. O,
You drunk and fucked-up munificence. O, Unshaven, Midnight,
Kindly lubricate my introduction to the unspeakable ring of chaos
You understand to be your life. You will surely pull the coil
      out of my car.
Oh no! He's going to show it to me—
God save the two of us, supernova.

PAUL ZARZYSKI

Zarzyski Meets the
Copenhagen Angel

Her Levis, so tight
I can read the dates on dimes
in her hip pocket. Miles City,
a rodeo Saturday night.
She smiles from a corner bar stool,
her taut lower lip, white and puffed,
pigtails braided like bronc reins.
She leads the circuit, chasing cans,
a barrel racer in love with her horse,
her snuff, and a 16 second run.
We dance close to LeDoux's "Daydream Cowboy."
I'm Zarzyski, rhymes with whiskey,
I tell her—a lover, a fighter,
a Polish bareback bronc rider.
And these Copenhagen kisses jump and kick
higher than ol' Moonshine, himself.

for Debbie Moore

RALPH POMEROY

The Leather Bar

Tonight, at the bar,
in the Members Only room,
the usual collection of aging 'cyclists'
lounge
wearing painfully tight jeans
elaborately arranged to show
maximum amount of cock and balls.
Even in summer a lot of them wear full leather.

Some are young—too young to be so pale,
so negative looking—and wear
that stupid expression resorted to
by those who try to appear indifferent.
They congratulate one another on some
new refinement in their get-ups—
a line of studs outlining their pockets,
a cleverly blocked cowboy hat, a pair
of real German Army boots.

Amid the greeting and badinage
a pool game goes: focus point—
because of the brilliant light bouncing
off its green field—
for involved nonchalance, exhibitions of
strained, tattooed muscles, 'baskets',
arching asses.

Cracks are made about someone wearing
mere shoes or—God forbid!—sneakers!
These are The Boys, The Fellas, The Guys.
So if someone ambiguous enters, sunny
from a lucky weekend, rested from enough sleep,
not drinking at the moment, in a good mood
really—

and is dresed for the heat
in an old open-necked shirt, loose pants
and sandals—
they look up, stir uneasily.

To them, he doesn't project a butch enough image.
The masses of long golden hair don't help.
His smoking a small, delicious cigar is a
gesture too filled with the 'wrong' style.
Immediate alienation.

But those who know him,
those who have been to bed with him,
know what they know.
He exchanges greetings with them—
of varying degrees of warmth.
And the sly, furtive, taken gazes
will pass back and forth all night
through the dark smoke.

Sizing up. Sizing up. A puzzle pieced
together: 'If A's been to bed with C and
seems to like him, and I've been to bed
with C and we got on fine, then maybe A
would work out for me . . .
And he knows G whom I've always wanted
to make-out with . . . He could tell me
what G digs . . . Guess I better move
over to a better spot so I'll be more
directly in his line of vision . . .'

The clock, which advertises beer,
says half-past two. Tomorrow's a working day.
Yet the bar stays full with a Great Number

yelling from the juke box.
No one wants the night to end yet.
Most hope to connect with someone—
impersonally, in a group, or maybe
personally,
one at a time.

Corsica Jean and Juanita's Palace

Girls weeping in the toilet at Strangers,
hair falling into their beer,
girls cursing into payphones,
girls waiting for a ride,
girls who stay drunk for a week,
girls with eyes staring back from some dead place
with caked blood on their lips,
girls with a story,
girls unbuttoning their coats
and leaning on the bar.
Love is a hard bread they've barely tasted
so if they ask for advice she'll tell them,
You've got to live with a bill stuck in your shoe.
Cab fare's the luxury of the brokenhearted.
All along Platt Street the darkness
is a prayer creeping over the Crosstown.
Too many nights and no sleep.
Coffee cup rings in all the book covers
laying around on countertops
like old friends who need no pampering,
who stay up all night to kill the wine.
She drags the blankets out onto the fire escape
to watch the last of the night
go sailing past, not exactly
a dreamboat, not a cruise for the queasy
of heart, salt in their beer,
out to a shore no river will wash clean.
Already the stars are blinking out
and all the girls standing out on some ledge
five stories up know she's no stranger
talking them down from the wrong side of the net.
And if they ask she'll tell them
there's no safety in numbers,
some rooms you can't find

your way out of for years,
still, nothing takes longer than you can bear it,
sometimes a man will take you
in his arms, let him look you in the eye,
let the sadness roll off of you
like the words from any jukebox song,
beautiful snake with nothing in its heart,
life is one lonely cab
everybody rides.

JOHN SKOYLES

The Fo'c'sle

You don't remember the tavern
down the block from where you worked,
how we waited for you to pass
and swooned behind the window
like guppies in love.

We slammed our glasses down
for no reason but to point out
we were alone with the mahogany
that would cradle our foreheads
late into the night.

Because you made us weak
in the knees, the guys
who follow boxing put it this way:
hit the body and the head will fall.
You don't remember.

But we imagine we're getting to you
as to the superstar who ignores
a ruckus in the bleachers
but still takes it home with him,
beyond us, where we never see how.

Drinking and Dancing

ELLEN BRYANT VOIGT

Dancing with Poets

"The accident" is what he calls the time
he threw himself from a window four floors up,
breaking his back and both ankles, so that walking
became the direst labor for this man
who takes my hand, invites me to the empty strip of floor
that fronts the instruments, a length of polished wood
the shape of a grave. *Unsuited for this world—*
his body bears the marks of it, his hand
is tense with effort and with shame, and I shy away
from any audience, but I love to dance, and soon
we find a way to move, drifting apart as each
effects a different ripple across the floor,
a plaid and a stripe to match the solid navy of the band.
And suddenly the band is getting better, so pleased
to have this pair of dancers, since we make evident
the music in the noise—and the dull pulse
leaps with unexpected riffs and turns, we can hear
how good the keyboard really is, the bright cresting
of another major key as others join us: a strict
block of a man, a formidable cliff of mind, dancing
as if melted, as if unhinged; his partner a gift of brave
elegance to those who watch her dance; and at her elbow,
Berryman back from the bridge, and Frost, relieved
of grievances, Dickinson waltzing there with lavish Keats,
who coughs into a borrowed handkerchief—all the poets of exile
and despair, unfit for this life, all those who cannot speak
but only sing, all those who cannot walk
who strut and spin until the waiting citizens at the bar,
aloof, judgmental, begin to sway or drum their straws
or hum, leave their seats to crowd the narrow floor
and now we are one body, sweating and foolish,

one body with its clear pathetic grace, not
lifted out of grief but dancing it, transforming
for one night this local bar, before we're turned back out
to our separate selves, to the dangerous streets and houses,
to the overwhelming drone of the living world.

MARK COX

Divorce

Like deeply chained buoys, languid and backlit by a neon sign,
they're still dancing to slow ones in the rear of the bar.

Old friends, as you said, come here to "do drinks," throw darts,
and "connect" with each other,

couples who have the feel of having known each other
for "longish" times,

before this place got popular with younger crowds.
Not old, of course, most aren't much older than you and I,

but still, with that weathered, companionable look
that marriage gives you

and five daiquiris can't take away —
like that tie you loosened, but could not bring yourself to undo

so you just slipped it over your head twice a day. And if now,
having made it, you're thinking, *Well, yet another glass raised*

against end-rhyme and Love's tailored, dry-cleaned noose;
another zipper lowered on upwardly mobile values,

all the better when I try to explain that I've never seen you
look so lonely in your whole half-life as a moment ago,

slipping past that bald guy — whose cigarette, incidentally,
you put out with your coat — playing darts back there,

dancing simultaneously and cheek-to-cheek with a wife
who'll need surgery to get out of her clothes.

One slow turn and he'll aim, throw the third and last,
then gently pat her ass

until she unlocks her arms, lets him go out a channel
between the pretzels and ivory-colored drink

she holds in respective hands.
For your birthday, all you wanted was to get to the bathroom,

and were making headway, until our waitress drove you against them.
And him, he swayed a little, then caught again

on the rhythm, reached down between their chests for matches
and craning his head behind hers relit the stub in his mouth,

while, as if you'd caused some immeasurable disturbance, seeming
to hold her even tighter for a moment,

dancing her away toward the round and tortured board,
not wanting to know if there was a hole in your life or not,

a black smudge to remember as meaning
one shouldn't, but has to, get close to love as that.

GILBERT SORRENTINO

Rose Room

Strange memorable objects:

caught in the most elegant turn of
the mind.

> In an old stupid film
> two stars enact the unwed
> couple
>
> in a roadhouse. They dance
> alone, to white swing music
> they embrace in static
> lust.
>
> The quality of light!
> in that scene, the absolute
> smell of summer out of
> fields, the distant haze
> implied thereon, these
>
> two stars danced into
> my youthful head.

So that, later, I saw a roadhouse
in that light, and danced in one,

the girl I was with and I
moved into that gentle occasion.

(Oh turn into summer, what
quality of American light
that is not bitter

is departed

Waltz of the Empty Roadhouse

Beautiful Berta aboard a bewildering barque
Broken and blue, busted, becalmed.

So, she sadly scans the thundering thalassa
Hugely heliotrope in hue.

Brown in the brisk breeze her breasts are bright and bronze
Brilliantly bruised by bum's boca.

Sadly she scans, so, the thundering thalassa
Hugely heliotrope in hue.

Bereft, benumbed, betrayed by the boys of el Bronx
Brandy and blackberries bore her.

So sadly she scans the thundering thalassa
Hugely heliotrope in hue.

PETER MICHELSON

hungry eye at the flin flon
(union pier, michigan)

Drummer, band, raucous roadhouse
rhythms—girls coiffured, manicured, petite
teenage chic, jeans.   Boys
indisputably Aryan,
clean.   Hausfraus—bland and
sagging—hoard their beer, wait glumly
for foxtrots, each other.
Schlitz flicks asteroids through
the dark, Hamm's glows eternal
Gitchee Gumee, and at the bar
the baptized hunch and over-
hang their stools.   GENTS and LADIES
glowing brutal orange diffuse
democratic auras of latrine . . .

From this you
rise and dance Diana,
Aphrodite—your

torso contours Bacchic
graces, such bones / such flesh transform

these mortal places, you
dance, smile and Cleopatra's walk

you mimic, laughing, mock
this myth, my need: your
magnitude of leg, of
hip, hair, and shoulder prove

a goddess once was real, you
bring a bronze to life, a
vision richer, older—your

sweeping poniard
fingers rake my
strings—ragged down below, above my demon sings

erotic
at the swirl your hair
in gloried orange and bluelit brings. . . . Your

sandaled instep arcs   and
flexing
rams my eye a rivet hotly

up your seam . . .
eyes like molten dreams
along your Levi seams find your

shadowed secret tautly
molded spots: that
moving marbles me, but
motion moves a motion if even only air—your

eyes ignite
a motion all men long to wear . . .   my

apparition are you
in this precarious night?   Or

are you incarnate here?
in this unlikely place,   in
this uncertain light

Tucson

A man was dancing with the wrong woman
in the wrong bar, the wrong part of town.
He must have chosen the woman, the place,
as keenly as you choose what to wear
when you dress to kill.
And the woman, who could have said no,
must have made her choice years ago,
to look like the kind of trouble
certain men choose as their own.
I was there for no good reason myself,
with a friend looking for a friend,
but I'm not important.
They were dancing close
when a man from the bar decided
the dancing was wrong. I'd forgotten
how fragile the face is, how fists too
are just so many small bones.
The bouncer waited, then broke in.
Someone wiped up the blood.
The woman began to dance
with another woman, each in tight jeans.
The air pulsed. My hands
were fidgety, damp.
We were Mexicans, Indians, whites.
The woman was part this, part that.
My friend said nothing's wrong, stay put,
it's a good fighting bar, you won't get hurt
unless you need to get hurt.

Deer Dancer

Nearly everyone had left that bar in the middle of winter except the hardcore. It was the coldest night of the year, every place shut down, but not us. Of course we noticed when she came in. We were Indian ruins. She was the end of beauty. No one knew her, the stranger whose tribe we recognized, her family related to deer, if that's who she was, a people accustomed to hearing songs in pine trees, and making them hearts.

The woman inside the woman who was to dance naked in the bar of misfits blew deer magic. Henry Jack, who could not survive a sober day, thought she was Buffalo Calf Woman come back, passed out, his head by the toilet. All night he dreamed a dream he could not say. The next day he borrowed money, went home, and sent back the money I lent. Now that's a miracle. Some people see vision in a burned tortilla, some in the face of a woman.

This is the bar of broken survivors, the club of shotgun, knife wound, of poison by culture. We who were taught not to stare drank our beer. The players gossiped down their cues. Someone put a quarter in the jukebox to relive despair. Richard's wife dove to kill her. We had to hold her back, empty her pockets of knives and diaper pins, buy her two beers to keep her still, while Richard secretly bought the beauty a drink.

How do I say it? In this language there are no words for how the real world collapses. I could say it in my own and the sacred mounds would come into focus, but I couldn't take it in this dingy envelope. So I look at the stars in this strange city, frozen to the back of the sky, the only promises that ever make sense.

My brother-in-law hung out with white people, went to law school with a perfect record, quit. Says you can keep your laws, your words. And practiced law on the street with his hands. He jimmied to the proverbial

dream girl, the face of the moon, while the players racked a new game.
He bragged to us, he told her magic words and that's when she broke,
  became human.
But we all heard his bar voice crack:
What's a girl like you doing in a place like this?

That's what I'd like to know, what are we all doing in a place like this?

☾

You would know she could hear only what she wanted to; don't we
all? Left the drink of betrayal Richard bought her, at the bar. What
was she on? We all wanted some. Put a quarter in the juke. We all
take risks stepping into thin air. Our ceremonies didn't predict this.
Or we expected more.

I had to tell you this, for the baby inside the girl sealed up with a lick of
hope and swimming into praise of nations. This is not a rooming
house, but a dream of winter falls and the deer who portrayed the
relatives of strangers. The way back is deer breath on icy windows.

The next dance none of us predicted. She borrowed a chair for the
stairway to heaven and stood on a table of names. And danced in the
room of children without shoes.

You picked a fine time to leave me, Lucille.
With four hungry children and a crop in the field.

And then she took off her clothes. She shook loose memory, waltzed
with the empty lover we'd all become.

She was the myth slipped down through dreamtime. The promise of
feast we all knew was coming. The deer who crossed through knots
of curse to find us. She was no slouch, and neither were we, watching.

The music ended. And so does the story. I wasn't there. But I imagined her like this, not a stained red dress with tape on her heels but the deer who entered our dream in white dawn, breathed mist into pine trees, her fawn a blessing of meat, the ancestors who never left.

ROBERT DANA

Bar Pastoral

Cowboys, jukes,
young queens,

apaches, and you,
Escudero. Snap

and crackle of
your brown eyes

as we dance
the hat dance,

ribbons streaming.
Not here, where

The White Noise
Blues Band rages

with loneliness,
and you give me

distance and a
politics of the heart,

iron with innocence.
But in a fiesta

of sunlight where
there's everything

to be said that's
been said before;

hard coin of
voices flickering

like silver;
a maracas of r's

whirring across
your tongue

something like love.

Last Call

"None of us will rest enough. . . ."

WILLIAM MATTHEWS

DIONISIO D. MARTÍNEZ

Folklore

A man walks into a bar is how the joke usually begins. Unless, of course, you happen to be the man and it happens to be your bar they're talking about. Then you find out that the bar is only a metaphor for one fear or another. You learn that the man is just an optional noun, used to give the sentence a sense of reality. The bar in the sentence is also a variable: given all the possible combinations, this specific series of events could've been shuffled differently to lead the man elsewhere. But the what-might've-been of the thing means nothing once you've reached a destination. Besides, a man needs a place where he can grab ahold of things that look like other things that last. So the bar becomes the soul of the sentence; and one common noun grabs ahold of the other, each of them hoping the other will last. A man walks into a bar. This bar. This man. At one time the joke was taught in the schools like algebra (let x be the man). It was analyzed by critics and used by just about everyone as a point of departure for the course of society. Now it has its place in the small talk of men in bars. A man, you say. Something led the man to the bar. Let x be the man. Algebra is a metaphor for all the unknowns a man fears and faces or thinks he faces on his way to a bar. So a man walks into a bar, you say to yourself as you walk into your bar and notice that everyone seems to be waiting for something. You say the first thing you always say when you walk in here. When you finish saying it, you notice that everyone is laughing as they clear the place for the night.

ALICIA OSTRIKER

Beer

After the store and the gas station close
There is still the bar,
With its real animal heads on the wall
Alert and thoughtful under their antlers,
Neither refusing nor rebuking you,
Its television they have tucked
Under the ceiling
Like a man holding a pingpong ball under his chin,
Where it yammers like a nervous female
Who uses her hands
More than a person needs to.

Your neighbors will be playing pool, sadly
And easily as they always do,
The teenage women hyped-up, more serious
Than their boyfriends,
The drunkards loud and wide
Like semis cruising down the interstate,
Their bellies stacked, a proud, rounded
Lifetime record of beer to show,
The snaky boys keeping their angular
Mouths shut, chalking their cues.

It could be raining or snowing outside.
Night after night somebody puts
"You Can Take This Job and Shove It"
On the jukebox, and you can hardly help
Loving the familiar bodies, the sounds,
The movements, and how everything goes together
For hours.

WILLIAM MATTHEWS

Another Beer

The first one was for the clock
and its one song
which is the song's name.

Then a beer for the scars in the table,
all healed in the shape of initials.

Then a beer for the thirst
and its one song we keep forgetting.

And a beer for the hands
we are keeping to ourselves.
The body's dogs, they lie
by the ashtray and thump
suddenly in their sleep.

And a beer for our reticence,
the true tongue, the one song,
the fire made of air.

Then a beer for the juke box.
I wish it had the recording
of a Marcel Marceau mime performance:
28 minutes of silence,
2 of applause.

And a beer for the phone booth.
In this confessional you can sit.
You sing it your one song.

And let's have a beer for whoever goes home
and sprawls, like the remaining sock,
in the drawer of his bed and repeats

the funny joke and pulls it
shut and sleeps.

And a beer for anyone
who can't tell the difference between
death and a good cry
with its one song.
None of us will rest enough.

The last beer is always for the road.
The road is what the car drinks
travelling on its tongue of light
all the way home.

BILLY COLLINS

Bar Time

In keeping with universal saloon practice,
the clock here is set fifteen minutes ahead
of all the clocks in the outside world.

This makes us a rather advanced group,
doing our drinking in the unknown future,
immune from the cares of the present,
safely harbored a quarter of an hour
beyond the woes of the contemporary scene.

No wonder such thoughtless pleasure derives
from tending the small fire of a cigarette,
from observing this glass of whiskey and ice,
the cold rust I am sipping,

or from having an eye on the street outside
when Ordinary Time slouches past in a topcoat,
rain running off the brim of his hat,
the late edition like a flag in his pocket.

Night Out

I have see you in the palms of my hands
late nights in the bar
                              just before the lights
are about to be turned on. You are powerful horses
by then, not the wrinkled sacks of thin, mewing
spirit,
          that lay about the bar early in the day
                                  waiting for minds and bellies.
You are the ones who slapped Anna on the back,
              told her to drink up
                that it didn't matter anyway.
You poured Jessie another Coors, and another one
                                              and another.
                      Your fingers were tight around hers
                  because she gave herself to you.
        Your voice screamed out from somewhere in the
darkness
                  another shot, anything to celebrate this deadly
        thing called living. And Joe John called out to bring
another round, to have another smoke, to dance dance it good
because tomorrow night is another year—
                                          in your voice.
              I have heard you in my ownself.
              And have seen you in my own past vision.
                              Your hearts float out in cigarette
    smoke, and your teeth are broken and scattered in my hands.
It doesn't end
For you are multiplied by drinkers, by tables, by jukeboxes
                  by bars.
You fight to get out of the sharpest valleys cut down into
the history of living bone.
                      And you fight to get in.
You are the circle of lost ones
                      our relatives.

You have paid the cover charge thousands of times over
with your lives
                    and now you are afraid

                              you can never get out.

The Remarkable Objectivity of Your Old Friends

We did right by your death and went out,
Right away, to a public place to drink,
To be with each other, to face it.

We called other friends—the ones
Your mother hadn't called—and told them
What you had decided, and some said

What you did was right; it was the thing
You wanted and we'd just have to live
With that, that your life had been one

Long misery and they could see why you
Had chosen that, no matter what any of us
Thought about it, and anyway, one said,

Most of us abandoned each other a long
Time ago and we'd have to face that
If we had any hope of getting it right.

Excuse for a Love Poem

It must have been the last drink
that made me feel like this.
A woman looking in a store window
stood the way you do;
a man drove a truck with a child
in his lap and somehow this touched me.

I saw everything with such affection,
it had to be that last drink
that made me think of love as a relief
instead of the relief of nothing to love,
and I flirted with a waitress to celebrate
but she never came back.

The women I thought about
always had someplace to go,
and guessing where you were today
only made me drunker:
the loveliness of being held,
the quiet in which you are reading.

DAVID RIVARD

The Wheel of the Hungry Is Turning

But no one in this bar hears,
Not one, & this bar, The
Buffet, flunks its name & feeds

No one, & none of us sees,
Though a young woman hikes up
Her blouse, lifts a child smaller

Than three months hypnotized
To her breast until baby
Sleeps again in her lap.

Smoking, eyeing the room, her
Husband straddles the next stool.
No one speaks to them, & she

Doesn't play Liar's Dice, can't
Shoot cutthroat, never mind pitch
Shuffleboard. This was her idea,

But right now she'd like to bolt.
Sure, sure, fine, says the husband—
Drunk, snarky—but why? can't you

Just relax? get loose, party
Some, you're all the time talking
You want to get out & meet

People, we don't see people.
Baby sleeps. Child of whatever
Impulses make these two stay, this

Middle-aged boy with beard
And dreadlocks, this woman pale
As her understandings, full

Of rocky good intentions.
These two stay. Now someone slams
Down a cup full of dice. Dice

Spill over the zinc counter,
Clattering, grungy, & over
Them swirl bar tunes, whispers, whoops,

Burps, sneezes, & avowals—
All the noises which drown out
The Wheel & keep it spinning,

Angry that it can't break us.

SILVIA CURBELO

Last Call

I know the man who eavesdrops
at the bar means no harm,
that he washes his hands of what is said,

that if his coffee grows cold
it isn't loneliness.

I know it isn't fear that leads
a beast to water, that sleep
comes down upon the blessed,

that when a good man drinks
the child inside him begins to close his eyes.

I know when the actress lifts her glass
that the movie continues, a role
she has slipped on like a raincoat
but there's no rain,

that in an avenue of trees and
perfect lawns the world is infinite.
The doorman leaning on somebody's
Cadillac loses track of time, his eyes fixed
on the beautiful map of anywhere.

And I know in small towns all over America
the jukeboxes are rigged,
that somewhere a man takes the wrong
woman in his arms and on a dance floor
a love song falls gently to its knees.

And I know the dark begins and ends
in a place we know by heart,

that sleep runs like a river through it,
and sooner or later we are all baptized.

By now the last insomniacs
are gathering their car keys and
drifting home to their books
and the all-night religious channel

and a voice climbs down an open window
across the dark tenements of salvation softly,
across the silent tract houses,

down among the sleepwalkers; their dreaming
eyes are shut.

List of Acknowledgments

Addonizio, Kim. "Intimacy." *Threepenny Review* (winter 1995): 39. Copyright © 1995 by Kim Addonizio. Reprinted with permission from the author.

Aleshire, Joan. "Pragmatists" and "The Man from the Restaurant." In *This Far*. Poetry series, vol. 27. Princeton, N.J.: *Quarterly Review of Literature*, 1987. Copyright © 1987 by Joan Aleshire. Reprinted with permission from *Quarterly Review of Literature*.

Ali, Agha Shahid. "The Keeper of the Dead Hotel." In *A Nostalgist's Map of America*. New York: W. W. Norton, 1991, 60–62. Copyright © 1991 Agha Shahid Ali. Reprinted with permission from W. W. Norton and Company, Inc.

Arnett, Carlen. "Morning at the Café du Monde." Copyright © 1997 by Carlen Arnett. Printed with permission from the author.

Baker, David. "8-Ball at the Twilite." In *Haunts*. Cleveland, Ohio: Cleveland State University Poetry Center. Copyright © 1995 by David Baker. Reprinted with permission from the author.

Balaban, John. "Kate and Gary's Bar, Red River, New Mexico." In *Words for My Daughter*. Port Townsend, Wash.: Copper Canyon Press, 1991, 47–48. Copyright © 1991 John Balaban. Reprinted with permission from Copper Canyon Press, P.O. Box 271, Port Townsend, WA 98368.

Barnett, Ruth Anderson. "Dixie Remembers the Runway," *New Letters* 60, no. 2 (spring 1994). Copyright © 1994 by Ruth Anderson Barnett. Reprinted with permission from the author.

Barnett, Ruth Anderson. "Mike's Bar, off I-5, North of Victorville." Copyright © 1997 by Ruth Anderson Barnett. Printed with permission from the author.

Baxter, Charles. "Fleetwood Café." In *Imaginary Paintings and Other Poems*. Potsdam, N.Y.: Paris Review Editions, 1989, 87. Copyright © 1989 by Charles Baxter. Reprinted with permission from the author.

Bell, Marvin. "A True Story." In *Drawn by Stones, by Earth, by Things That Have Been in the Fire*. New York: Atheneum, 1984, 161–63. Copyright © 1984 by Marvin Bell. Reprinted with permission from the author. Later published in *New and Selected Poems*.

Berger, Bruce. "Smoke and Mirrors." In *Facing the Music*. Lewiston, Idaho: Confluence Press, 1995, 23. Copyright © 1995. Reprinted with permission from Confluence Press, at Lewis-Clark State College, Lewiston, ID.

Berger, Bruce. "Dining Late." *Light* (spring 1992): 23. Copyright © 1992 by Bruce Berger. Reprinted with permission from the author.

Berger, Bruce. "Motel Room Curtains." Copyright © 1997 by Bruce Berger. Printed with permission from the author.

Black, Sophie Cabot. "Report from Nirvana." *Bomb* (spring 1994). Copyright © 1994 by Sophie Cabot Black. Reprinted with permission from the author.

Bosselaar, Laure-Anne. "Letter from Jake's Place, Durango." *Nimrod* 39, no. 1 (winter 1995): 94. Copyright © 1995 by Laure-Anne Bosselaar. Reprinted with permission from the author.

Bosselaar, Laure-Anne. "Parentheses." Copyright © 1997 by Laure-Anne Bosselaar. Printed with permission from the author.

Brock-Broido, Lucie. "The Letter L" and "Kid Flash." In *A Hunger*. New York: Alfred A. Knopf, 1988, 32, 29. Copyright © 1988 by Lucie Brock-Broido. Reprinted by permission of Alfred A. Knopf, Inc.

Brown, Kurt. "Wide World of Sports" and "Two Restaurants." Copyright © 1997 by Kurt Brown. Printed with permission from the author.

Budy, Andrea Hollander. "Poem for My Brother, Manager of a Go-Go Bar in Roselle Park, New Jersey." In *House without a Dreamer*. Brownsville, Ore.: Story Line Press, 1993, 65–66. Copyright © 1993 by Andrea Hollander Budy. Reprinted with permission from Story Line Press.

Byrkit, Rebecca. "The Only Dance There Is." In *zealand*. Tucson: SUN/gemini Press, 1995, 19. Copyright © 1995. Reprinted with permission from SUN/gemini Press. Originally appeared in *New England Review*.

Carpenter, William. "At the Foxtrot Motel" and "The Husbands." In *Rain*. Boston: Northeastern University Press, 1985, 37–39, 35–36. Copyright © 1985 by William Carpenter. Reprinted with permission from the author.

Carver, Raymond. "In the Lobby of the Hotel del Mayo." In *Ultramarine*. New York: Random House, 1986, 75–76. Copyright © 1986 by Tess Gallagher. Reprinted by permission of Tess Gallagher.

Carver, Raymond. "Reading Something in the Restaurant." In *Where Water Comes Together with Other Water*. New York: Random House, 1984, 122–23. Copyright © 1984. Reprinted by permission of Tess Gallagher.

Claman, Elizabeth. "Café Macondo." *Hubbub* 8, no.2 (winter 1990–1991). Copyright © 1990 by Elizabeth Claman. Reprinted with permission from the author.

Claman, Elizabeth. "La Terrasse des Marronniers." Copyright © 1997 by Elizabeth Claman. Printed with permission from the author.

Collins, Billy. "Bar Time." In *The Apple That Astonished Paris*. Fayetteville: University of Arkansas Press, 1988, 48. Copyright © 1988 by Billy Collins. Reprinted with permission from University of Arkansas Press.

Cooper, Wyn. "Fun." In *The Country of Here Below*. Boise, Idaho: Ahsahta Press, 1987, 20–21. Copyright © 1987 by Wyn Cooper. Reprinted with permission from the author.

Cooper, Wyn. "Bad Manners." Copyright © 1997 by Wyn Cooper. Printed with permission from the author.

Cox, Mark. "Inhospitable." Copyright © 1996 by Mark Cox. Reprinted by permission of the author. First published in *Leaning House Poets*.

Cox, Mark. "Divorce" and "The Angelfish." In *Smoulder*. Lincoln, Mass.: David R. Godine, Publisher, 1989, 35–36. Copyright © 1989 by Mark Cox. Reprinted with permission from David R. Godine, Publisher.

Curbelo, Silvia. "Summer Storm." *Linden Lane* 9, no. 3 (1990). Copyright © 1990 by Silvia Curbelo. Reprinted with permission from the author.

Curbelo, Silvia. "Corsica Jean and Juanita's Palace." In *The Geography of Leaving*. Eugene, Ore.: Silverfish Review Press, 1991. Copyright © 1991 by Silvia Curbelo. Reprinted with permission from the author.

Curbelo, Silvia. "Last Call." *Tampa Review*, no. 4 (1991): 10. Copyright © 1991 by Silvia Curbelo. Reprinted with permission from the author.

Dana, Robert. "Bar Pastoral." In *Yes, Everything*. Chicago: Another Chicago Press, 1994, 27–28. Copyright © 1994 by Robert Dana. Reprinted with permission from Another Chicago Press.

Daniels, Jim. "Short-order Cook" and "Ted's Bar and Grill." In *Places / Everyone*. Madison: University of Wisconsin Press, 1985, 61, 15–16. Copyright © 1985 by Jim Daniels. Reprinted with permission from University of Wisconsin Press.

Deming, Alison Hawthorne. "Saturday, J.'s Oyster Bar" and "Caffe Trieste." In *Science and Other Poems*. Baton Rouge: Louisiana State University Press, 1994, 41, 7. Copyright © 1994 by Alison Hawthorne Deming. Reprinted by permission of Louisiana State University Press.

Dickey, James. "Adultery." In *Falling, May Day Sermon and Other Poems*. Middletown, Conn.: Wesleyan University Press, 1981, 29–30. Copyright © 1981 by James Dickey. Reprinted by permission of University Press of New England.

Dobyns, Stephen. "Tenderly." In *Velocities*. New York: Penguin, 1994. Copyright © 1994 by Stephen Dobyns. Reprinted with permission from Penguin, a division of Penguin Books USA, Inc.

Dugan, Alan. "To a Red-Headed Do-Good Waitress." In *New and Collected Poems 1961–1983*. New York: Ecco Press, 1983, 82. Copyright © 1983 by Alan Dugan. Reprinted with permission from The Ecco Press.

Dunn, Stephen. "Belly Dancer at the Hotel Jerome." In *New and Selected Poems 1974–1994*. New York: W. W. Norton, 1994, 74. First published in *A Circus of Needs*. Pittsburgh: Carnegie Mellon University Press, 1978. Copyright © 1978 by Stephen Dunn. Reprinted by permission of the author and W. W. Norton and Company, Inc.

Dunn, Stephen. "Tucson." In *Loosestrife*. New York: W. W. Norton, 1996, 22. Copyright © 1996 by Stephen Dunn. Reprinted with permission from the author and W. W. Norton and Company, Inc. First published in *Crazyhorse*.

Emanuel, Lynn. "Outside Room Six," "Discovering the Photograph of Lloyd, Earl, and Priscilla," and "The Night Man at the Blue Lite." In *The Dig*. Champaign:

University of Illinois Press, 1992, 10, 109, 9. Copyright © 1992–1994 by Lynn Emanuel. Reprinted with permission from University of Illinois Press.

Espada, Martín. "Transient Hotel Sky at the Hour of Sleep." In *City of Coughing and Dead Radiators*. New York: W. W. Norton, 1993, 52–54. Copyright © 1993 by Martín Espada. Reprinted with permission from W. W. Norton and Company, Inc.

Ferlinghetti, Lawrence. "Café Notre Dame" and "*Ristorante Vittoria*, Milan." In *Over All the Obscene Boundaries*. New York: New Directions, 1980, 23, 51–52. Copyright © 1980 by Lawrence Ferlinghetti. Reprinted by permission of New Directions Publishing Corporation.

Ferlinghetti, Lawrence. "Holiday Inn Blues." In *Landscapes of Living and Dying*. New York: New Directions, 1979, 18–20. Copyright © 1979 by Lawrence Ferlinghetti. Reprinted by permission of New Directions Publishing Corporation.

Finkel, Donald. "Fall in the Equinox Café." In *The Detachable Man*. New York: Atheneum, 1984. Copyright © 1984 by Donald Finkel. Reprinted with permission from the author.

Frost, Carol. "Patience." *TriQuarterly*, no. 96 (spring/summer 1996): 199. Copyright © 1995 by Carol Frost. Reprinted with permission from the author.

Gander, Forrest. "Draft of the Smoky Life." In *Lynchburg*. Pittsburgh: University of Pittsburg Press, 1993, 28–29. Copyright © 1993. Reprinted by permission of University of Pittsburgh Press.

Garcia, Richard. "Hôtel des Grandes Écoles." In *The Flying Garcias*. Pittsburgh: University of Pittsburg Press, 1993, 58–59. Copyright © 1993. Reprinted by permission of University of Pittsburgh Press.

Graham, Jorie. "In the Hotel." In *Materialism*. Hopewell, N. J.: Ecco Press, 1995, 56–58. Copyright © 1995 by Jorie Graham. Reprinted with permission from The Ecco Press.

Greenberg, Alvin. "Old Sonny." In *Why We Live with Animals*. Minneapolis: Coffee House Press, 1990. Copyright © 1990 by Alvin Greenberg. Used by permission of the publisher.

Gunn, Thom. "Cafeteria in Boston." In *The Man with Night Sweats*. New York: Farrar, Straus and Giroux, 1992, 48–49. Copyright © 1992 by Thom Gunn. Reprinted by permission of Farrar, Straus and Giroux, Inc.

Hacker, Marilyn. "Elysian Fields." In *Winter Numbers*. New York: W. W. Norton, 1994, 31–32. Copyright © 1994 by Marilyn Hacker. Reprinted with permission from W. W. Norton and Company, Inc. Originally appeared in *Paris Review*.

Harjo, Joy. "Deer Dancer." In *Mad Love and War*. Middletown, Conn.: Wesleyan University Press, 1990, 5–6. Copyright © 1990 by Joy Harjo. Reprinted by permission of University Press of New England.

Harjo, Joy. "Night Out." In *She Had Some Horses*. New York: Thunder's Mouth Press, 1983, 21. Copyright © 1983 by Joy Harjo. Reprinted by permission of Thunder's Mouth Press.

Haug, James. "Terminal Hotel" and "Pool Is a Godless Sport." In *The Stolen Car.* Amherst: University of Massachusetts Press, 1989, 7, 26. Copyright © 1989 by James Haug. Reprinted with permission from University of Massachusetts Press.

Hawkins, Gary. "The Manager." Copyright © 1997 by Gary Hawkins. Printed with permission from the author.

Haxton, Brooks. "Bar Story." In *The Sun at Night.* New York: Alfred A. Knopf, 1995, 42–44. Copyright © 1995 by Brooks Haxton. Reprinted by permission of Alfred A. Knopf, Inc.

Herrera, Juan Felipe. "Iowa Blues Bar Spiritual." In *Night Train to Tuxtla.* Tucson: University of Arizona Press, 1994, 120–22. Copyright © 1994 by Juan Felipe Herrera. Reprinted with permission from the author. First published in *New England Review.*

Hiestand, Emily. "Moon Winx Motel." Copyright © 1997 by Emily Hiestand. Printed with permission from the author.

Hirsch, Edward. "Hotel Window." *The New Republic* 210, no. 22 (May 30, 1994): 40. Copyright © 1994 by Edward Hirsch. Reprinted with permission from the author.

Hoagland, Tony. "Travellers." In *Sweet Ruin.* Madison: University of Wisconsin Press, 1993, 55–56. Copyright © 1993. Reprinted with permission from the University of Wisconsin Press.

Hugo, Richard. "Dancer at Kozani's," "The Only Bar in Dixon," "What the Brand New Freeway Won't Go By," and "Death of the Kapowsin Tavern." In *Making Certain It Goes On: The Collected Poems of Richard Hugo.* New York: W. W. Norton, 1984, 72–73, 212, 86–87, 102. Copyright © 1965, 1970, 1973 by Richard Hugo. Copyright © 1984 by the Estate of Richard Hugo. Reprinted with permission from W. W. Norton and Company, Inc. "The Only Bar in Dixon" originally appeared in *The New Yorker.*

Hull, Lynda. "Night Waitress" In *Ghost Money.* Amherst: University of Massachusetts Press, 1986, 14–15. Copyright © 1986 by Lynda Hull. Reprinted with permission from University of Massachusetts Press. First published in the *Missouri Review.*

Hull, Lynda. "Jackson Hotel." *The New Yorker* (April 1, 1985): 44. Copyright © 1985 by Lynda Hull. Reprinted by permission of estate.

Hyde, Lewis. "Hotel with Birds." In *This Error Is the Sign of Love.* Minneapolis: Milkweed Editions, 1988, 56–58. Copyright © 1988 by Lewis Hyde.

Inez, Colette. "Cleveland Summer of Nickel Tips." In *Eight Minutes from the Sun.* Upper Montclair, N. J.: Saturday Press, 1983, 15. Copyright © 1983 by Colette Inez. Reprinted with permission from Saturday Press, Inc.

Inez, Colette. "Short Order Cook, Blue Mill Diner." Copyright © 1997 by Colette Inez. Reprinted with permission from the author. First published in *Corduroy.*

Inez, Colette. "Mitch." Copyright © 1997 by Colette Inez. Reprinted with permission from the author. First published in *Red Clay Reader.*

Irwin, Mark. "The Western Hotel." Copyright © 1997 by Mark Irwin. Printed with permission from the author.

Johnson, Denis. "All-Night Diners." In *The Veil*. New York: Alfred A. Knopf, 1987, 42–44. Copyright © 1987 by Denis Johnson. Reprinted with permission from Alfred A. Knopf, Inc.

Johnson, Denis. "A Woman." In *The Incognito Lounge*. New York: Random House, 1982, 38–39. Copyright © 1982 by Denis Johnson. Reprinted with permission from Random House.

Johnson, Denis. "In a Rented Room." In *The Man among the Seals*. Iowa City: Stone Wall Press, 1969, 39. Copyright © 1969 by Denis Johnson. Reprinted with permission from Stone Wall Press.

Johnson, Markham. "The All-Night Diner." In *Collecting the Light*. Tallahassee: University Press of Central Florida, 1993, 36. Copyright © 1993 by Markham Johnson. Reprinted with permission from the author.

Jones, Rodney. "On the Bearing of Waitresses." In *Transparent Gestures*. New York: Houghton Mifflin, 1989, 16–17. Copyright © 1989 by Rodney Jones. Reprinted by permission of Houghton Mifflin Company. All rights reserved.

Kennedy, X. J. "In a Prominent Bar in Secaucus One Day." In *Nude Descending a Staircase*. New York: Doubleday, 1961, 33–34. Copyright © 1961 by X. J. Kennedy, renewed. Reprinted by permission of Curtis Brown Ltd.

Kinnell, Galway. "The Man on the Hotel Room Bed." In *When One Has Lived a Long Time Alone*. New York: Alfred A. Knopf, 1990, 20–21. Copyright © 1990 by Galway Kinnell. Reprinted by permission of Alfred A. Knopf Inc.

Koestenbaum, Phyllis. "Admission of Failure." *Epoch* 40, no. 1 (1991): 19. Copyright © 1991 by Phyllis Koestenbaum. Reprinted with permission from the author. Also published in *The Best American Poetry 1992*.

Kooser, Ted. "Boarding House." In *Sure Signs*. Pittsburgh: University of Pittsburgh Press, 1980, 68. Copyright © 1980. Reprinted by permission of University of Pittsburgh Press.

Krysl, Marilyn. "Gem Inn, Kandy." Copyright © 1997 by Marilyn Krysl. Printed with permission from the author.

Kumin, Maxine. "The Chambermaids in the Marriott in Mid-Morning." In *Looking for Luck*. New York: W. W. Norton, 1992, 79. Copyright © 1992 by Maxine Kumin. Reprinted with permission from W. W. Norton and Company, Inc. Originally published in *American Poetry Review*.

Kunitz, Stanley. "The Illumination." In *Passing Through: The Later Poems New and Selected*. New York: W. W. Norton, 1970, 29–30. Copyright © 1970 by Stanley Kunitz. Reprinted with permission from W. W. Norton and Company, Inc.

Laux, Dorianne. "Landrum's Diner, Reno." In *What We Carry*. Brockport, N. Y.: BOA Editions Limited, 1995, 56. Copyright © 1995 by Dorianne Laux. Reprinted with the permission of BOA Editions, Ltd., 92 Park Avenue, Brockport, NY 14420.

Larsen, Wendy Wilder. "Lunch with My Ex." Copyright © 1997 by Wendy Wilder Larsen. Reprinted with permission from the author. An earlier version of this poem first appeared in the *Seattle Poetry Review*.

Lavieri, Jon. "The Beacon of Winchester County." *Abiko Quarterly* 16, no. 13 1/2 (winter 1993–1994). Copyright © 1993 by Jon Lavieri. Reprinted with permission from the author.

Lavieri, Jon. "Meditation on Lloyd's Diner" and "Breakfast at the Golden Egg Cafe." Copyright © 1997 by Jon Lavieri. Printed with permission from the author.

Levine, Philip. "The Midget." In *Not This Pig*. Middletown, Conn.: Wesleyan University Press, 1968, 58–60. Copyright © 1968 by Philip Levine. Reprinted by permission of University Press of New England.

Levine, Philip. "The Seven Doors." *TriQuarterly* (spring/summer 1996): 85. Copyright © 1996 by Philip Levine. Reprinted with permission from the author.

Lewis, Lisa. "The Accident." In *The Unbeliever*. Madison: University of Wisconsin Press, 1994, 26–28. Copyright © 1994. Reprinted with permission from University of Wisconsin Press.

Lux, Thomas. "Motel Seedy." In *The Drowned River*. New York: Houghton Mifflin, 1990. Copyright © 1990 by Thomas Lux. Reprinted with permission from the author.

Lux, Thomas. "One Meat Ball." *Black Warrior Review* 21, no. 2 (spring/summer 1995): 124–25. Copyright © 1990 by Thomas Lux. Reprinted with permission from the author.

Martínez, Dionisio D. "Folklore" and "Dancing at the Chelsea." In *History as a Second Language*. Columbus: Ohio State University Press, 1993, 56, 37–40. Copyright © 1993 by Ohio State University Press. Reprinted with permission from the publisher.

Matthews, William. "Mingus at The Showplace" and "Mingus at The Half Note." In *Time and Money*. New York: Houghton Mifflin, 1995, 5, 18. Copyright © 1995 by William Matthews. Reprinted by permission of Houghton Mifflin Company. All rights reserved.

Matthews, William. "Another Beer." In *Sleek for the Long Flight*. New York: Random House, 1971. Copyright © 1971 by William Matthews. Reprinted with permission from the author.

Matthews, William. "A Story Often Told in Bars: The *Reader's Digest* Version." *The New Yorker* (1993). Copyright © 1993 by William Matthews. Reprinted with permission from the author.

Matthews, William. "Lunch in Hell." *Tar River Poetry* (fall 1995): 15. Copyright © 1995 by William Matthews. Reprinted with permission from the author.

McCarriston, Linda. "The Stardust." In *Eva-Mary*. Evanston, Ill.: Northwestern University Press, 1991, 38–39. Copyright © 1991 by Linda McCarriston. Reprinted with permission from TriQuarterly Books / Northwestern University Press.

McGrath, Campbell. "Angels and the Bars of Manhattan." In *American Noise*. New York: Ecco Press, 1993, 13–16. Copyright © 1993 by Campbell McGrath. Reprinted with permission from The Ecco Press.

McHugh, Heather. "Spilled," "Gig at Big Al's," and "The Most." In *Hinge and Sign: Poems, 1968–1993*. Middletown, Conn.: Wesleyan University Press, 1994, 202–3, 103, 104. Copyright © 1994 by Wesleyan University Press. Reprinted by permission of University Press of New England.

Merwin, W. S. "The Hotel-Keepers." In *The Drunk in the Furnace*. New York: Macmillan, 1960, 51–53. Copyright © 1956, 1957, 1958, 1959, 1960 by W. S. Merwin. Reprinted with permission of Georges Borchardt, Inc., for the author.

Michelson, Peter. "hungry eye at the flin flon." In *The Eater*. Athens, Ohio: Swallow Press, 1972, 36–37. Copyright © by Peter Michelson. Reprinted with permission from the author.

Mitchell, Susan. "The Hotel by the Sea," "A Story," and "Feeding the Ducks at the Howard Johnson Motel." In *Rapture*. New York: HarperCollins, 1992, 6–8, 38–40, 49–50. Copyright © 1992 by Susan Mitchell. Reprinted with permission from HarperCollins.

Mullen, Laura. "Museum Garden Café." In *The Surface*. Urbana: University of Illinois Press, 1991, 32. Copyright © 1991 by Laura Mullen. Reprinted with permission from University of Illinois Press.

Murphy, Peter E. "At the Meadowlands Hotel." Copyright © 1997 by Peter E. Murphy. Printed with permission from the author.

Murphy, Peter E. "At the Waterloo Hotel." *The Ledge*, no. 20 (summer 1996). Copyright © 1996 by Peter E. Murphy. Reprinted with permission from the author.

Olsen, William. "The Oasis Motel." In *Vision of a Storm Cloud*. Evanston, Ill.: Northwestern University Press, 1996, 79–80. Copyright © 1996 by William Olsen. Reprinted with permission from Northwestern University Press.

Orr, Gregory. "Transients Welcome." In *Burning the Empty Nests*. New York: Harper and Row, 1973, 16. Copyright © 1973 by Gregory Orr. Reprinted with permission from the author.

Orr, Gregory. "Hotel St. Louis, New York City, Fall 1969." In *New and Selected Poems*. Middletown, Conn.: Wesleyan University Press, 1988, 85–87. Copyright © 1988 by Gregory Orr. Reprinted with permission from the author.

Ostriker, Alicia. "Beer." In *The Imaginary Lover*. Pittsburgh: University of Pittsburg Press, 1986, 6. Copyright © 1986. Reprinted by permission of University of Pittsburgh Press.

Pape, Greg. "In the Bluemist Motel," "Desert Motel before Dawn," and "Coldburn Vertigo." In *Sunflower Facing the Sun*. Iowa City: University of Iowa Press, 1992, 16–17, 3–4, 5–8. Copyright © 1992 by Greg Pape. Reprinted by permission of University of Iowa Press.

Peacock, Molly. "Goodbye Hello in the East Village." In *Original Love*. New York: W. W. Norton, 1995, 86–88. Copyright © 1995 by Molly Peacock. Reprinted with permission from W. W. Norton and Company, Inc.

Pettit, Michael. "Mr. Ho's." In *American Light*. Athens: University of Georgia Press, 1984, 8. Copyright © 1984 by Michael Pettit. Reprinted with permission from University of Georgia Press.

Pettit, Michael. "Vanna White's Bread Pudding." Copyright © 1997 by Michael Pettit. Printed with permission from the author.

Pomeroy, Ralph. "The Leather Bar." In *The Penguin Book of Homosexual Verse*. New York: Penguin Books, 1983. Copyright © 1983 by Ralph Pomeroy. Reprinted with permission from the author.

Porter, Browning. "The Poet Flexes His Magnanimity." *Poetry East* 39 (fall 1994): 72. Copyright © 1994 by Browning Porter. Reprinted with permission from the author.

Raab, Lawrence. "Romanticism." In *Other Children*. Pittsburgh: Carnegie Mellon University Press, 1987, 16. Copyright © 1987 by Lawrence Raab. Reprinted with permission from Carnegie Mellon University Press.

Rector, Liam. "The Remarkable Objectivity of Your Old Friends." In *American Prodigal*. Brownsville, Ore.: Story Line Press, 1994, 33. Copyright © 1994 by Liam Rector. Reprinted with permission from Story Line Press.

Reinhard, John. "For the Barmaid Unhappy with the Size of Her Breasts." In *Burning the Prairie*. Minneapolis, Minn.: New Rivers Press, 1988, 73–74. Copyright © 1988 by John Reinhard. Reprinted with permission from New Rivers Press.

Rhodes, Martha. "In This New England Inn's Bed." Copyright © 1997 by Martha Rhodes. Printed with permission from the author.

Rivard, David. "The Road Out" and "The Wheel of the Hungry Is Turning." In *Torque*. Pittsburgh: University of Pittsburgh Press, 1988, 19, 45–46. Copyright © 1988. Reprinted by permission of University of Pittsburgh Press.

Sadoff, Ira. "At the Half Note Café." In *Emotional Traffic*. Lincoln, Mass.: David R. Godine, 1989, 77–78. Copyright © 1989 by Ira Sadoff. Reprinted by permission of David R. Godine, Publisher, Inc.

Sadoff, Ira. "The Bus Boy." Copyright © 1997 by Ira Sadoff. Printed with permission from the author.

St. Germain, Sheryl. "Fanks." In *Making Bread at Midnight*. Austin, Tex.: Slough Press, 1989, 21. Copyright © 1989 by Sheryl St. Germain. Reprinted with permission from Slough Press.

St. John, David. "Hotel Sierra" and "Desire." In *Study for the World's Body: Selected Poems*. New York: HarperCollins, 1994. Copyright © 1994 by David St. John. Reprinted with permission from HarperCollins Publishers, Inc.

Santos, Sherod. "The Enormous Aquarium." In *The Southern Reaches*. Middletown, Conn.: Wesleyan University Press, 1989, 37–38. Copyright © 1989 by Sherod Santos. Reprinted with permission from University Press of New England.

Sears, Peter. "The Tablecloth Explanation." *Ploughshares* 1, no. 4 (1973): 25. Copyright © 1973 by Peter Sears. Reprinted with permission from the author.

Sears, Peter. "Harvey Wallbanger." Copyright © 1997 by Peter Sears. Reprinted with permission from the author. First published in *Chowder Review*.

Sears, Peter. "Lip's Lounge." Copyright © 1997 by Peter Sears. Reprinted with permission from the author. First published in *Portland Review*.

Seidel, Frederick. "Pressed Duck." In *Poems: 1959–1979*. New York: Alfred A. Knopf, 1980, 75–76. Copyright © 1980 by Frederick Seidel. Reprinted by permission of Alfred A. Knopf, Inc.

Shinder, Jason. "Waitress." In *Every Room We Ever Slept In*. Bronx, N. Y.: Sheep Meadow Press, 1993, 30. Copyright © 1993 by Jason Shinder. Reprinted with permission from Sheep Meadow Press.

Simic, Charles. "Paradise Motel." In *A Wedding in Hell*. San Diego: Harcourt Brace, 1994, 10. Copyright © 1994 by Charles Simic. Reprinted by permission of Harcourt Brace and Company.

Simic, Charles. "The Partial Explanation." In *Charon's Cosmology*. New York: George Braziller, 1977, 3. Copyright © 1977 by Charles Simic. Reprinted by permission of George Braziller, Inc.

Simic, Charles. "Hotel Insomnia." In *Hotel Insomnia*. New York: Harcourt Brace Jovanovich, 1992, 12. Copyright © 1992 by Charles Simic. Reprinted by permission of Harcourt Brace and Company.

Simic, Charles. "For the Sake of Amelia." In *Unending Blues*. San Diego: Harcourt Brace Jovanovich, 1986, 12. Copyright © 1986 by Charles Simic. Reprinted by permission of Harcourt Brace and Company.

Simon, Michael. "The Bar of Forgetfulness." Copyright © 1997 by Michael Simon. Printed with permission from the author.

Simpson, Louis. "Out of Season." In *Caviare at the Funeral*. New York: Franklin Watts, 1980, 82–85. Copyright © 1980 by Louis Simpson. Reprinted with permission from Grolier Publishing Company.

Skoyles, John. "Excuse for a Love Poem," "Kilcullen & Murray's," and "The Fo'c'sle." In *A Little Faith*. Pittsburgh: Carnegie Mellon University Press, 1981, 17, 39, 42. Copyright © 1981 by John Skoyles. Reprinted with permission from Carnegie Mellon University Press.

Smith, Charlie. "Redneck Riviera." In *The Palms*. New York: W. W. Norton, 1993, 22. Copyright © 1993 by Charlie Smith. Reprinted by permission of W. W. Norton and Company, Inc.

Smith, Dave. "At the Greek's Bar." In *Night Pleasures: New and Selected Poems*. Chester Springs, Pa.: Bloodaxe Books, 1971. Copyright © 1971 by Dave Smith. Reprinted with permission from the author.

Snodgrass, W. D. "Leaving the Motel." In *Selected Poems: 1957–1987*. New York: Soho Press, 1987, 89. Copyright © 1987 by W. D. Snodgrass. Reprinted with permission from Soho Press.

Solomon, Mark. "These Are the Streets." *TriQuarterly*, no. 91 (fall 1994): 185. Copyright © 1994 by Mark Solomon. Reprinted with permission from the author.

Sorrentino, Gilbert. "Rose Room," and "Waltz of the Empty Roadhouse." In *Selected Poems: 1958–1980*. Santa Rosa, Calif.: Black Sparrow Press, 1981, 113, 227. Copyright © 1981 by Gilbert Sorrentino. Reprinted with permission from Black Sparrow Press.

Speakes, Richard. "Sweet Dreams at the Silver Slipper Tavern." Copyright © 1991 by Richard Speakes. Reprinted with permission from the author. An earlier version was published in *Passages North* 12, no. 1 (summer 1991).

Stanton, Maura. "The All-Night Waitress." In *Snow on Snow*. Pittsburgh: Carnegie Mellon University Press, 1975, 12–13. Copyright © 1975 by Maura Stanton. Reprinted with permission from Carnegie Mellon University Press.

Stern, Gerald. "There Is Wind, There Are Matches." In *The Red Coal*. Boston: Houghton Mifflin, 1981, 70–71. Copyright © 1981 by Gerald Stern. Reprinted by permission of Hougton Mifflin Company. All rights reserved.

Stern, Gerald. "At Bickford's." In *Lucky Life*. Boston: Houghton Mifflin, 1977, 3–4. Copyright © 1977 by Gerald Stern. Reprinted with permission from author. Also printed in *Leaving Another Kingdom: Selected Poems*.

Stone, Ruth. "The Latest Hotel Guest Walks Over Particles that Revolve in Seven Other Dimensions Controlling Latticed Space." In *Second Hand Coat*. Cambridge, Mass.: Yellow Moon Press, 1991, 40–41. Copyright © 1991 by Ruth Stone. Reprinted with permission from Yellow Moon Press, P.O. Box 1316, Cambridge, MA 02238. (617) 776-2230.

Swenson, Karen. "Surface and Structure: Bonaventure Hotel, Los Angeles." In *A Sense of Direction*. New York: The Smith, 1989, 85. Copyright © 1989 by Karen Swenson. Reprinted with permission from The Smith.

Swenson, Karen. "The Landlady in Bangkok." In *The Landlady in Bangkok*. Port Townsend, Wash.: Copper Canyon Press, 1994, 55–56. Copyright © 1994 by Karen Swenson. Reprinted with permission from Copper Canyon Press, P.O. Box 271, Port Townsend, WA, 98368.

Tate, James. "At the Days End Motel." *Field*, no. 52 (spring 1995): 26. Copyright © 1995 by James Tate. Reprinted with permission from the author.

Twichell, Chase. "The Hotel du Nord." In *The Odds*. Pittsburgh: University of Pittsburgh Press, 1986, 34. Copyright © 1986. Reprinted by permission of University of Pittsburgh Press.

Twichell, Chase. "Worldliness" and "Chanel No. 5." In *Perdido*. New York: Farrar, Straus and Giroux, 1991, 9–13, 44–45. Copyright © 1991 by Chase Twichell. Reprinted by permission of Farrar, Straus and Giroux.

Van Walleghen, Michael. "Hamburger Heaven." In *Blue Tango*. Urbana: University of Illinois Press, 1989, 84–85. Copyright © 1989 by Michael Van Walleghen. Reprinted with permission from University of Illinois Press.

Voigt, Ellen Bryant. "Dancing with Poets." In *The Lotus Flowers*. New York: W. W. Norton, 1987, 69–70. Copyright © 1987 by Ellen Bryant Voigt. Reprinted with permission from W. W. Norton and Company, Inc.

Walcott, Derek. Sections III and XXXVI in *Midsummer*. New York: Farrar, Straus and Giroux, 1984. Copyright © 1984 by Derek Walcott. Reprinted by permission of Farrar, Straus and Giroux, Inc.

Watson, Ellen Doré. "A Hotel by Any Other Name." Copyright © 1997 by Ellen Doré Watson. Printed with permission from the author.

Wier, Dara. "The Buckhorn Exchange." Copyright © 1997 by Dara Wier. Printed with permission from the author.

Williams, C. K. "Second Persons: Café de L'Abbaye." In *Flesh and Blood*. New York: Farrar, Straus and Giroux, 1987. Copyright © 1987 by C. K. Williams. Reprinted by permission of Farrar, Straus and Giroux, Inc.

Williams, C. K. "The Regulars." In *Poems 1963–1983*. New York: Farrar, Straus and Giroux, 1988. Copyright © 1988 by C. K. Williams. Reprinted with permission from Farrar, Straus and Giroux, Inc.

Wood, Renate. "The Hotel." In *Raised Underground*. Pittsburgh: Carnegie Mellon University Press, 1991, 13. Copyright © 1991 by Renate Wood. Reprinted with permission from Carnegie Mellon University Press.

Wood, Susan. "Knowing the End." In *Campo Santo: Poems by Susan Wood*. Baton Rouge: Louisiana State University Press, 1991, 26–27. Copyright ©1991 by Susan Wood. Reprinted by permission of Louisiana State University Press.

Wright, Charles. "Bar Giamaica, 1959–60." In *The World of the Ten Thousand Things: Poems 1980–1990*. New York: Farrar, Straus and Giroux, 1990, 39. Copyright © 1990 by Charles Wright. Reprinted by permission of Farrar, Straus and Giroux, Inc.

Wright, James. "Old Man Drunk." In *Saint Judas*. Middletown, Conn.: Wesleyan University Press, 1959, 6–7. Copyright © 1959 by James Wright. Reprinted by permission of University Press of New England.

Wright, James. "Hotel Lenox." In *Two Citizens*. New York: Farrar, Straus and Giroux, 1970, 29. Copyright © 1970 by James Wright. Reprinted by permission of Farrar, Straus and Giroux, Inc.

Wunderlich, Mark. "Take Good Care of Yourself." Copyright © 1997 by Mark Wunderlich. Printed with permission from the author. First published in *The Paris Review*.

Zarzyski, Paul. "Zarzyski Meets the Copenhagen Angel" and "Zarzyski Stomachs the Oxford Special with Zimmer at the Ox Bar & Grill." In *Roughstock Sonnets*. Reno: University of Nevada Press, 1989. Copyright © 1989 by Paul Zarzyski. Reprinted with permission from the author.

Zimmer, Paul. "Romance." In *Big Blue Train*. Fayetteville: University of Arkansas Press, 1993, 46. Copyright © 1993 by Paul Zimmer. Reprinted by permission of University of Arkansas Press. Originally published in *The Southern Review*.

About the Editors

KURT BROWN is the founder of the Aspen Writers' Conference and Writers' Conferences and Festivals (a national association of directors), past editor of *Aspen Anthology*, and past president of the Aspen Literary Foundation.

His poems have appeared in many periodicals, including the *Ontario Review*, the *Berkeley Poetry Review*, the *Seattle Review*, the *Southern Poetry Review*, the *Massachusetts Review*, and the *Indiana Review*.

He is the editor of three annuals, *The True Subject* (Graywolf Press, 1993), *Writing It Down for James* (Beacon Press, 1995), and *Facing the Lion* (Beacon Press, 1996), which gather outstanding lectures from writers' conferences and festivals as part of the Writers on Life and Craft series.

He is also the editor of *Drive, They Said: Poems about Americans and Their Cars*, published by Milkweed Editions in 1994.

LAURE-ANNE BOSSELAAR grew up in Belgium where she published a collection of French poems, *Artémis* (1982). She holds an MFA from the Warren Wilson College Program for Writers.

Among other publications, her poems have appeared in the *Massachusetts Review*, the *Denver Quarterly*, the *International Quarterly*, *Ploughshares*, the *Sycamore Review*, *The Spoon River Poetry Review*, and *Nimrod*.

Two of her poems were chosen to be included in *The Writing Path 1: Poetry and Prose from Writers' Conferences* published by the University of Iowa Press (1995).

A collection of her poems, *The Hour between Dog and Wolf*, is scheduled for publication by BOA Editions in May 1997.

The editors are married and live in Cambridge, Massachusetts.

Author Index

Interior design by Will Powers
Typeset in Electra
by Stanton Publication Services, Inc.
Printed on acid-free Glatfelter paper
by Edwards Brothers, Inc.

More poetry anthologies from Milkweed Editions:

Clay and Star:
Contemporary Bulgarian Poets
Translated and edited
by Lisa Sapinkopf and Georgi Belev

Drive, They Said:
Poems about Americans and Their Cars
Edited by Kurt Brown

Looking for Home:
Women Writing about Exile
Edited by Deborah Keenan and Roseann Lloyd

Minnesota Writes: Poetry
Edited by Jim Moore and Cary Waterman

Mixed Voices:
Contemporary Poems about Music
Edited by Emilie Buchwald and Ruth Roston

Mouth to Mouth:
Poems by Twelve Contemporary Mexican Women
Edited by Forrest Gander

Passages North Anthology:
A Decade of Good Writing
Edited by Elinor Benedict

The Poet Dreaming in the Artist's House:
Contemporary Poems about the Visual Arts
Edited by Emilie Buchwald and Ruth Roston

This Sporting Life:
Contemporary American Poems
about Sports and Games
Edited by Emilie Buchwald and Ruth Roston

MILKWEED EDITIONS publishes with the intention of making a humane impact on society, in the belief that literature is a transformative art uniquely able to convey the essential experiences of the human heart and spirit.

To that end, Milkweed publishes distinctive voices of literary merit in handsomely designed, visually dynamic books, exploring the ethical, cultural, and esthetic issues that free societies need continually to address.

Milkweed Editions is a not-for-profit press.

811.508   Night out.
NIG

$14.95